Transforming Primary QTS

Teaching Bilingual
and EAL Learners in Primary Schools

Transforming Primary QTS

Teaching Bilingual and EAL Learners in Primary Schools

Jean Conteh

Series editor: Alice Hansen

Los Angeles | London | New Delhi
Singapore | Washington DC

Learning Matters
An imprint of SAGE Publications Ltd
1 Oliver's Yard
55 City Road
London EC1Y 1SP

SAGE Publications Inc.
2455 Teller Road
Thousand Oaks, California 91320

SAGE Publications India Pvt Ltd
B 1/I 1 Mohan Cooperative Industrial Area
Mathura Road
New Delhi 110 044

SAGE Asia-Pacific Pte Ltd
3 Church Street
#10-04 Samsung Hub
Singapore 049483

Editor: Amy Thornton
Development Editor: Jennifer Clark
Production controller: Chris Marke
Project management: Deer Park Productions,
Tavistock
Marketing manager: Catherine Slinn
Cover design: Wendy Scott
Typeset by: PDQ Typesetting Ltd
Printed by: MPG Books Group, Bodmin, Cornwall

MIX
Paper from
responsible sources
FSC® C018575

First published in 2012

Library of Congress Control Number: 2012938953

British Library Cataloguing in Publication data

A catalogue record for this book is available from the British Library

ISBN 978 0 85725 861 8
ISBN 978 0 85725 749 9 (pbk)

Contents

The Author

Jean Conteh is a senior lecturer in the School of Education at the University of Leeds, where she teaches on the PGCE Primary course and on MA courses. She has worked in many countries and is a very experienced teacher educator. She has published widely in the field of EAL in primary education, both for teachers and for academic audiences. Her research focuses on ways to promote success for those pupils who are often labelled 'disadvantaged' in our education system, and covers the role of language in teaching and learning in primary classrooms and the expertise and professional roles of bilingual teachers.

Series Editor

Alice Hansen

Alice Hansen is the Director of Children Count Ltd where she is an educational consultant. Her work includes running professional development courses and events for teachers and teacher trainers, research and publishing. Alice has worked in education in England and abroad. Prior to her current work she was a primary mathematics tutor and the programme leader for a full-time primary PGCE programme at the University of Cumbria.

Acknowledgements

I am grateful to the following former students who have contributed to this book by providing examples of children's work and classroom activities:

Shannele Cowban
Anna Grant
Sarah Kent
Lian Montgomery

I wish to thank Tracey Burns of the OECD for the use of the cartoon on page 40.

I also wish to thank my colleague, Linda Palmer for her perceptive reading of drafts and helpful comments.

Extract from *The Iron Man* by Ted Hughes reproduced by kind permission of Faber.

Introduction

The overarching aim of this book is to situate EAL centrally in the context of excellent primary education. One of its key arguments is that the principles of good provision for all learners underpin the development of good practice that meets the distinctive needs of bilingual and EAL learners. Two of the main themes in the book illustrate this point: the importance of academic language and the need to revitalise the role of oral language and language learning across the curriculum. Both underpin the thinking that has informed the development of the long-awaited new primary curriculum and are key to good-quality provision for EAL learners.

The book raises issues and challenges misconceptions about language teaching and learning generally and about EAL learners in particular. Such misconceptions have, in the past, contributed to what could be termed a 'deficit' model of EAL learners, constructing them as children on the margins of mainstream education with problems that needed to be sorted out before they could be included. This book argues strongly for a positive perspective on diversity and in particular a view of language diversity as a resource and an opportunity for learning, for all children. It is my hope that the book will instil in our next generation of primary teachers enthusiasm and passion for an aspect of their work which offers in return a great deal of professional reward and satisfaction.

The prime audience for this book is people who have chosen to become primary teachers, no matter what route they are taking, from the well-established, university and college-based PGCE and Degree level courses to the vast array of school-based training programmes that are being developed round the country. It is also relevant for other audiences, such as tutors in initial teacher education, newly-qualified teachers (NQTs) and their mentors, teachers working with EAL learners in primary schools and those engaged in continuing professional development (CPD), and possibly working towards higher qualifications. It provides a theory-informed, accessible, comprehensive source of practical guidance for meeting the needs of children categorised as EAL learners in primary schools. As such, it is perhaps the first book of its kind, and is very timely. Not only are the numbers of children in our schools who speak and write other languages besides English growing rapidly year by year, but the nature of their prior experiences and thus of their learning needs is becoming more and more diverse.

Structure and organisation of the book

The book is in two parts. The first part comprises Chapters 1–3 and the second Chapters 4–7. In between the two parts there is a set of principles, which are intended to show how theory and practice always need to be integrated in considering the best provision for bilingual and EAL learners, indeed any learners.

Part 1: Understanding EAL learners – theories of learning and language

The chapters in the first part of the book provide theoretical and contextual information to frame the more practical ideas that form the second part of the book. Essentially, it aims to provide:

- a contextualisation of the issues, including a consideration of the development of EAL in England and illuminative vignettes of children who would come under the umbrella of 'EAL';
- essential theoretical information, with discussion of the practical implications, about the role of language in learning generally and the development and learning of pupils who can be defined as 'EAL' and 'bilingual'.

Chapter 1: Introducing bilingual and EAL learners begins by providing some facts and figures, which explain how our present 'superdiverse' society in England has come about. Following this, it aims to answer the question, 'who are EAL learners?' by offering vignettes of individual children, using terminology from policy documentation. This section covers children in five categories, showing the need to be aware of the complexities and uncertainties in understanding their strengths and needs. The final section raises some common myths and misconceptions about language diversity and learning, which are addressed at different points in the book and returned to at the end.

Chapter 2: All about language provides a theoretical overview of language, culture and identity. It explains what is involved in the 'functional approach' to understanding grammar and texts, showing the value of this for teaching and learning. The second section provides an introduction to sociocultural theories of learning, in which talk is a central element, and argues for the importance of talk in working with bilingual and EAL learners in particular.

Chapter 3: What does it mean to be bilingual? addresses relevant theories about bilingualism and their practical implications in making the best provision for bilingual and EAL learners. Beginning with an overview of global contexts, it moves on to consider research related to bilingualism and education, in particular the work and ideas of Jim Cummins. The chapter ends by emphasising the importance for pupils' success in school of understanding the nature of home and community learning experiences that many bilingual and EAL learners bring to school.

Part 1 closes by articulating some 'key principles' for promoting success for EAL learners, which are illuminated with practical examples in Chapters 4–7.

Part 2: Promoting learning – practical approaches for bilingual and EAL learners

Based on the key principles identified in the first part of the book, the second part (Chapters 4–7) focuses on practical classroom issues. It covers the important themes of planning, classroom strategies, resources, assessment and making links with home and community contexts.

Chapter 4: Planning across the curriculum for bilingual and EAL learners provides guidance for planning language-focused activities across the curriculum using a framework (The Cummins' quadrant) which makes clear the ways that planning can support the progression of learning to higher, more academic levels. There are sections on planning for collaborative talk, on including new arrivals in your lessons and on planning for using home languages in bilingual children's learning.

Chapter 5: Strategies and resources for promoting learning across the curriculum is a very full chapter which provides a wealth of ideas and suggestions for developing activities that link language learning and content learning, use children's 'funds of knowledge' and exploit the rich resource of stories to promote language and content learning.

Chapter 6: Assessing bilingual and EAL learners across the curriculum begins by suggesting some principles for assessing EAL and bilingual learners. It then moves to a discussion of standardised assessments of attainment and the issues they raise for bilingual and EAL learners. It stresses the importance of assessment for learning (AFL) and introduces a framework, developed by the **National Association for Language Development in the Curriculum (NALDIC),** which is designed to identify the distinctive features of bilingual development in listening, speaking, reading and writing. The possible confusions between language needs and special needs are addressed and the chapter ends with some practical advice on assessment for learning, observing pupils and consulting with parents.

Chapter 7: Conclusions: synthesising learning and moving on revisits the myths identified in Chapter 1 and the principles at the end of Part 1. It invites readers to reflect on their developing professional knowledge and suggests ways of moving on in order to extend and strengthen their professional expertise related to bilingual and EAL learners.

In line with other titles in the *Learning Matters Transforming Primary QTS* series, the book contains the following structural and study support features.

- *Learning outcomes* – a list of objectives is given at the start of each chapter, which are reviewed (with self-assessment questions) at the end of the chapter.
- *Research focus* – each chapter contains relevant research focus sections. In Chapters 4–7, there is some cross-reference to the research discussed in Chapters 2 and 3.
- *Activities* and discussion points are included throughout each chapter, linked to the ideas being discussed.
- *Case studies* are included in each chapter, to illustrate the general points being made and to help relate the ideas directly to classrooms. Across the book as a whole, all curriculum subjects are represented in the case studies.
- An annotated list of *further reading* and a full list of *references* are included at the end of each chapter.
- A *glossary* is included at the end of the book where all terms highlighted in bold in the body of the text are explained.
- *Model answers* to the learning outcomes questions are also provided.

Part 1
Understanding EAL learners – theories of learning and language

1. Introducing bilingual and EAL learners

> ## Learning Outcomes
>
> This chapter will help you to achieve the following learning outcomes:
>
> - develop understanding of the importance of recognising and reflecting on your own views on language diversity and ethnicity for you as a primary teacher;
> - gain awareness of the history of language and cultural diversity in England;
> - develop awareness of the diverse range of experiences and knowledge that bilingual and EAL learners bring to their primary classrooms in England.

Introduction

This chapter introduces you to the children you will be teaching who come under the umbrella term of 'EAL learners'. It raises questions about how we define and label attributes such as 'ethnicity' and challenges you to consider your own views and perceptions of these issues. It begins by providing some background information about the cultural and language diversity of British society. Then, through a set of vignettes of individual children, you will gain a sense of the rich diversity of the social and cultural experiences that many bilingual and EAL learners bring to their mainstream classrooms. One of the main aims of this chapter is to help you, as a beginning teacher, to understand the importance of recognising and valuing all the knowledge and experience that your bilingual and EAL learners bring with them to school. This is crucial, if you are to help them become successful learners in the mainstream system. Interspersed through the chapter there are questions and activities to help you to think further through the ideas that you will read about, as well as begin to think practically about their implications for your own practice in different classrooms. There are some suggestions for further reading at the end of the chapter.

These are the main sections and subsections of the chapter.

1. Defining difference
- Behind the facts and figures
- 'Superdiversity' in England

2. Who are 'EAL learners'?
- Advanced bilingual learners – Yasmin
- New to English children – Stefan and Jan
- Asylum-seekers and refugees – Umaru
- Isolated learners – Radia

● Sojourners – Hamida

3. Language diversity and learning – some myths and misconceptions

1. Defining difference

1.1 Behind the facts and figures

Research Focus

Since 2009, the Department for Education has collected information about the languages spoken by children in schools as part of the annual schools' census data. In 2011, the figures showed that about 16.8% of children in mainstream primary and 12.3% in secondary schools in England were identified as learners with 'EAL' (English as an additional language). It is not easy to find a figure for the total number of languages currently spoken by children in schools in England, but it is thought to be about 350 (BBC, 2007). The proportion of ethnic minority children is different from those defined as 'EAL'; currently this is 21.4% for primary schools and 25.5% for secondary schools (Department for Education, 2011a). The data on ethnicity come from the national census, which is done every ten years. The most recent census was undertaken in 2011, and the categories for ethnicity used are shown in the box below. The national census has never collected information about the languages that people speak.

The percentages for ethnic minority children are much higher than those for language diversity, so it is clear that there are many ethnic minority groups in England for whom English is *not* an additional language. But it is also clear that many children can be defined as *both* EAL and ethnic minority, because they belong to an ethnic minority group and also speak another language besides English. It is important to understand, especially for children such as those in this second group, that language knowledge and cultural knowledge are interlinked. This idea is discussed further in Chapter 2, as well as the implications for teaching. There are also children who would ethnically be part of the 'white' majority but who could actually be defined as 'EAL', because they do not have English as their first language and their families are from Europe or other parts of the world.

Activity 1.1
Who are you?
These are the categories of ethnicity used in the 2011 national census. Look at them and think about the following questions.

1. Did you complete the most recent census? If so, which category did you place yourself in? If not, which category would you place yourself in?

2. Could you place yourself into more than one category?
3. Do you find it difficult to place yourself, and if so, why?
4. Would it be difficult to place anyone you know?
5. Would it be difficult to place any children you teach or have worked with?
6. How do you think these categories were arrived at?

A. White
- British
- English/Welsh/Scottish/Northern Irish/British Irish
- Gypsy or Irish traveller
- Any other White background

B. Mixed/multiple ethnic groups
- White and Black Caribbean
- White and Black African
- White and Asian
- Any other Mixed

C. Asian/Asian British
- Indian
- Pakistani
- Bangladeshi
- Chinese
- Any other Asian background

D. Black/African/Caribbean/Black British
- African
- Caribbean
- Any other Black/African/Caribbean background

E. Other ethnic group
- Arab
- Any other ethnic group

Despite the ever-increasing numbers of children from different ethnic and language backgrounds in our schools, the vast majority of teachers in England are still from 'white British or English' backgrounds and do not speak other languages besides English. This means that most teachers who have children in their classes who speak other languages do not share those languages. This can sometimes feel like quite a challenge, on top of everything else you need to know about and be able to do as a teacher. Vivian Gussin Paley, in her book *White teacher*, describes her experiences as a 'white majority' teacher in a school with increasing numbers of children from diverse backgrounds. She soon realised that, in order to understand their needs and make the best provision for them, she had to understand more about her own identity and how it influenced her attitudes to her pupils. She concludes:

Those of us who have been outsiders understand the need to be seen exactly as we are and to be accepted and valued. Our safety lies in schools and societies in which faces with many shapes can feel an equal sense of belonging. Our children must grow up knowing and liking those who look and speak in different ways, or they will live as strangers in a hostile land.

(pp. 131–2)

Ethnicity is a very hard concept to define, and because we often talk about 'ethnic minorities' we sometimes think of it as a term only relevant for people who are different from ourselves and can be thought of as belonging to a 'minority' group. Of course, the reality is that we all have ethnicity. We all belong to different ethnic, cultural and social groups. But ethnicity is only one part of what makes us who we are. In thinking about your role as a teacher, it is more helpful to think about the notion of **identity**, and all the personal and social attributes that this entails. As suggested in Chapter 2, it is vital that you understand how your personal identity is an important aspect of your professional identity as a teacher, especially when you are teaching children from different language and cultural backgrounds to yourself. You need to understand the importance to you of your own ethnicity, language knowledge and other aspects of your personal makeup in helping you understand the needs of the children you will be teaching. As Gussin Paley argues, in this way, you will be able to develop positive, trustful relationships with the children you teach and with their families.

The following activity will help you to think about your 'ethnicity' as part of your identity – in other words, who you are.

Activity 1.2
How does it feel to be different?
You can do this activity on your own. But it would be better if you could do it as a group discussion task, with some of your fellow trainees, or colleagues in a school setting.

- First, think about how you would define your identity. Is it enough just to think about your 'ethnic background' as defined in the categories of the census? What other aspects of your identity are important to you? Where your family comes from might be an important part of your identity, but what else might count for you?
- Make a list of 6–8 attributes that you would say were important aspects of your identity.
- Can you think of a time when you were made to feel different and that you did not belong? This could have been when you were a child, or as an adult in a work situation or in a social context. What did you feel was different about you? How would the quote from Vivian Gussin Paley reflect your feelings? Write a few sentences about how it felt to feel different and perhaps excluded.

1.2 'Superdiversity' in England

In about 120 AD, soldiers from the Roman Empire built a fort on the river Tyne and named it Arbeia (see Arbeia Fort, 2011). Some historians think they named it after their homelands in what are now Syria, Libya and Spain. Britain has always been multicultural and multilingual – a small island which has experienced successive waves of migration from all over the world. The English language reflects this, as it contains words from all the languages of the people that have come to this island and enriched its vocabulary over the centuries.

Over recent years, with the growth of the European Union (EU) as well as more global events, the population of England has changed greatly. The addition to the EU of the 'A8 accession countries' in 2004 and more recent changes have meant that people travel much more than they used to. It has become quite normal for people from Poland, the Czech Republic, Slovakia and other eastern European countries to come to England to work, and then return to their countries of origin or move on elsewhere. This has been described as 'circular migration', and is a worldwide phenomenon. In many British cities now, there are what have been called '**superdiverse**' communities. People with vastly different languages, histories, cultural and social backgrounds and religions live side by side. Sometimes, new migrants arrive and join with communities from their countries of origin that have lived in the city for generations.

Case Study: A superdiverse corner shop

This photo of a corner shop in a Yorkshire city shows clearly the effects of 'superdiversity' on everyday life in a typical community.

Figure 1.1 Shop front in a 'superdiverse' city

→

A Lithuanian heritage family-owned the shop from the 1950s until they sold it to a Pakistani heritage family in the 1980s. A few years ago, this family sold the shop to a Polish man. He put up a new sign, covering the old Lithuanian name. He kept the small 'halal meat' logos from the Pakistani heritage owners at the edges of the sign to show that he still provides meat for the local Muslim community. He also sells phone cards to customers from all over the world. He placed a bright yellow banner in the shop window (at the bottom right of the picture) to show how he catered for the changing community around the shop: 'Everyone welcome English, Arabic, Kurdish, Polish, Slovakia', it says. There are now many multilingual communities like this in cities all over England, where many of our EAL children live.

Also, as we see below, an increasing number now also live in towns or villages where they may be very few other bilingual children.

Activity 1.3
Language and cultural diversity in school

If you have a placement in a school where there are children learning English as an additional language, try to find out the following information.

1. How many children in school are defined as 'EAL learners'?
2. How many different languages are spoken by children in the school?
3. How does the school find out about and record the languages?
4. Does the school have a policy for EAL or language diversity?
5. How are EAL issues managed in the school?

If you cannot undertake this activity in your placement school, see if you could arrange a visit to a school where it would be possible to do it.

2. Who are 'EAL learners'?

Sometimes the term 'EAL' is applied only to children who are actually better thought of as 'new to English'. In reality, 'EAL' is an umbrella term for many different groups of children who bring a vast range of experience and knowledge of languages, cultures, schooling and literacies to their mainstream classrooms. The title of this book refers to 'bilingual and EAL learners' to make the point that we cannot think of the children whose learning we are considering as one, uniform group. Different terms have been used over the years in policies and strategy documents to describe the EAL learners you may meet in your classrooms. Here is a list of them.

- Learners who are second and third generation members of settled ethnic minority communities (advanced bilingual learners).
- Learners who are recent arrivals and new to English, some of whom have little or no

experience of schooling, and others who are already literate in their first languages (children new to English).

- Learners whose education has been disrupted because of war and other traumatic experiences (asylum-seekers and refugees).

- Learners who are in school settings with little prior experience of bilingual children (isolated learners).

- Learners whose parents are working and studying and are in England for short periods of time (sojourners).

> ## Activity 1.4
> **Thinking about bilingual and EAL learners**
> Before you read the vignettes that follow, think about the children in your current class, or one you have recently taught. Do you think any of them would fit into any of the groups listed above?
>
> Write a list of the names of the children, and identify which group you think each would belong to.

What follow are five vignettes that will help you to understand something about the children that belong to each of the groups listed above and to develop your understanding about who could be defined as 'EAL learners'.

2.1 Advanced bilingual learners – Yasmin

Yasmin, is eight years old and in a Year 3 class in a large, multilingual primary school in a city very like the one where the photo above was taken. Most of her classmates are from similar backgrounds to herself. She represents the biggest group in our list of different categories of EAL learners. She was born in England, the granddaughter of a man who arrived from the Kashmir area of Pakistan forty or fifty years ago to work in the woollen mills in the city. Yasmin is multilingual. English is her dominant language, so 'EAL' is not really a helpful way to describe her. As well as English, she speaks Punjabi and Urdu. She is also **multiliterate** (Datta, 2007). With her sisters and female cousins, she is learning the Koran in Arabic from a Muslim teacher who visits her home. Her brothers go to the local mosque, which is in a converted cinema close to their house. Her mum is teaching her to read and write Urdu, their heritage national language. All these languages have important, but different, roles to play in her life. While English may be the most important, there is no sign that the other languages are fading away. Indeed, the signs are that they will continue to be important for Yasmin and her community (see Chapter 3). Punjabi is the foreign language most commonly spoken by British people, with over half a million speakers. Children whose families originate from Bangladesh would have very similar histories, with Bengali and Sylheti as their community languages. Bengali is the second most commonly spoken foreign language by British people (Wikipedia, 2011).

Yasmin is doing very well in school so far. She is very talkative and keen to answer questions. At the end of Year 2, in the KS1 **Standardised Attainment Tasks (SATs)** she attained level 2 in English and level 3 in mathematics. Her dad helps her a lot in mathematics at home, teaching her the multiplication tables in Punjabi. Her mother and aunts do a lot of sewing, and Yasmin is very good at this and other practical activities. When she was younger, her grandma told her and her siblings lots of stories from Pakistan, in Punjabi. The children loved this and knew many of the stories by heart. Yasmin's reception teacher found out about this, and encouraged the children to tell the stories in school, with the bilingual teaching assistant helping to interpret for her. This had a big benefit for Yasmin's literacy, as it helped her to understand story structures and the kinds of language found in stories, which is different from spoken language. Children like Yasmin are exactly those whom Deryn Hall describes as 'living in two languages' (Hall et al. 2001), and who are discussed in Chapter 3.

2.2 New to English children – Stefan and Jan

Stefan and Jan are both ten years old, and in the same Year 5 class in a small Roman Catholic school in a big city in the north of England. They have both been attending the school for a couple of years, having arrived from Poland at almost the same time with their families. About 40% of the pupils in the school are from Pakistani-heritage backgrounds, and the numbers of children from Poland, the Czech Republic and Slovakia are steadily growing – currently it is about 10%, that is 2–3 children per class. Stefan and Jan's class teacher is a bit puzzled by the two boys. She checked the school records, and noticed that, since coming to the school, both new to English, their progress has been very different. They seemed to start off from a relatively similar position in relation to their knowledge of English. Both have become fairly confident and fluent in spoken English over the two years they have been in the school. They can answer questions in class, hold conversations with their teachers and their peers and take part in social activities in school. But, while Stefan has made good progress with reading and writing and is beginning to perform in assessments at similar levels to his peers, Jan is struggling. He has taken part in various intervention activities, but never seems to be able to catch up with Stefan or his other classmates.

The class teacher is considering what can be done to support Jan to help him catch up before he encounters the KS2 SATs in Year 6. She wonders whether yet another intervention activity is the answer. In studying part-time for her MA, she comes across the work of Cummins (see Chapter 3) and other writers on bilingualism. She finds their ideas about the links between languages in children's learning very intriguing and decides to find out a little about Stefan and Jan's knowledge of other languages, especially their home language, Polish. To her surprise and interest, she finds out that Stefan is an accomplished reader and writer of Polish, and that he regularly attends the Polish Saturday school in the city, where children study Polish to GCSE and A level. Jan, on the other hand, can only read and write a little Polish – his early schooling in Poland was disrupted because of his family situation. He went to the Saturday class for a short while, but then dropped out.

As an experiment, the teacher asks Stefan if he can bring some of his Polish books into school and tell the class about some of the things he does in the Saturday school. Stefan's dad comes along too, and tells the class a story in Polish, which Stefan translates into English. The visit is a huge success. Afterwards, the teacher notices how Jan seems much more enthusiastic and motivated. So she decides to give the children opportunities, from time to time, to work together in same-language groups where they can discuss things with each other, using their home languages and then report back or write in English (see section 2 of Chapter 4 for more information about planning and organising groupwork). As time goes on, Jan's reading and writing slowly begin to improve, while his confidence steadily grows.

2.3 Asylum-seekers and refugees – Umaru

Umaru is eleven years old and in Year 6. He came to England as a baby with his mother, Jenneh, who had had to escape from her home town in Sierra Leone, when it was overrun by fighting during the civil war that ended about ten years ago. His father was a solicitor and his mother an administrator in a large secondary school in the town. At first, Umaru and his mother lived temporarily in bed and breakfast accommodation in London, and after 18 months they moved to a small town in the north-west of England where Jenneh had a friend. Other friends helped with accommodation and Jenneh found a job in a supermarket. They settled fairly well, although they were the target of racial abuse for a while. But they had lost touch with Umaru's father because of the unsettled situation in Sierra Leone. Jenneh applied for political asylum and, after a long struggle, she gained it.

Though they had been in their new home for two years, by the time Umaru began school, their future was still uncertain. Events in Sierra Leone had calmed and Jenneh had made contact with her family, but Umaru's father had died. All the problems she faced were a great strain on Jenneh and she became depressed. The school was a fairly small, Church of England school with very few non-white pupils. At first, Umaru was a well-behaved little boy and he made a good impression on his teachers. He was very polite and spoke good English, as Jenneh had been careful to teach him because English is the official language of Sierra Leone. However, the teachers knew nothing about his home country apart from the awful events that were sometimes shown on television. This made the teachers feel sorry for Umaru, and they did not push him very hard in his work. There were other ethnic minority children in the school, but none from Africa. As time went on, Umaru's attendance at school was sometimes irregular as he had to stay at home to look after his mother when she felt unable to go to work. His school work suffered and he did not make many friends. He did not do well in the KS1 SATs at the end of KS1, and was placed in a SEN group, where he became very withdrawn. He got further and further behind in his work, and his behaviour also began to suffer as his anxiety about his mother grew. No one at school knew of his home situation. Now that he has reached Year 6, his prospects of attaining level 4 in the SATs look slim. His work in school is clearly not meeting expectations, nor is it reflecting his true ability.

2.4 Isolated learners – Radia

Radia is in Year 4 in a primary school in a village near to a small city in the south west of England. The family have been living in England for five years altogether. She has been attending the school for two years, after moving to the village with her family when her father began a job at the local university, where he had recently completed his PhD. When the family first arrived in England from their home country, Algeria, they lived in the city, near the university. Radia attended a large, busy, multilingual primary school where she had some friends whose parents were also students. She did very well and was happy. When the job offer came, Radia's parents decided to move to the village in order to have a bigger house and garden and – they hoped – better schooling for their three children, of whom Radia is the eldest.

All is not going as well as they hoped. Radia's mother is finding it lonely living in the village with no Algerian friends nearby. Although her neighbours are very pleasant, none of them visit her as regularly as she would like, and she often spends days alone with her young child. She takes the two older children to school every day and would like to be able to talk to their teachers more than she does. But she never seems to be able to engage them in conversation. Radia has not settled very well into school. She misses the friends she made in her old school, and has not really made any new friends in the village school. She is the only 'EAL' pupil in her class, and one of only eight or ten in the whole school, all of whom are from well-educated, middle-class backgrounds, some from Islamic countries in the Middle East and others from China. Their parents are either students or former students, like Radia's, or professionals working for companies in the city.

The school has taken steps to find out how to support their new pupils – one teacher has been given responsibility for their induction, and went on a training course, which was part of the *New arrivals excellence programme* (Department for Education, 2011b). But she did not find anything very relevant for the pupils coming to the village school. They all seem to be very fluent in English so language does not seem to an issue for them. One of the strategies recommended on the course was to form good relationships with the children's parents, and she would like to be able to do this. But when she meets them as they bring their children to school and come to collect them, she finds it difficult to think of ways to generate conversations with them. She has not had much prior experience of people from different cultural backgrounds. She raises this in a staff meeting, and this leads to a long discussion. One of the outcomes is a decision to organise a social event to give parents an opportunity to meet their children's teachers and see something of the work they do in class. This proves a great success, and greatly helps the processes of communication in the school.

2.5 Sojourners – Hamida

Hamida is five years old and in Year 1 in a large, mainly white school in a prosperous city in the south of England. She arrived with her family from Saudi Arabia in the city at the start of the school year. Her father is doing a PhD at the university, and her mother also has plans to study, once childcare arrangements are made for Hamida and her two younger brothers. Hamida speaks Arabic, and is also learning to read and write it in a Saturday class run by the wife of another Saudi Arabian student. Her parents are very concerned that she maintains her skills in Arabic, as they will be returning home in three or four years' time. They are also very keen that she learns to speak English – indeed, this was one of the main reasons why they decided to bring her to England with them, rather than leaving her at home with relatives, as other students have done with their children. They want her to learn 'proper' English so that she speaks as far as possible with a **Received Pronunciation** (**RP**) accent, which will afford her high status in Saudi Arabia. They also, quite naturally, want her to retain her Muslim identity, and hope that the school are aware of, and sensitive to, Islamic rules and practices.

The class that Hamida has joined comprises mostly 'white British' children, though there is one other bilingual child, whose parents are students, like Hamida's. He is from Indonesia and – like Hamida – his family is Muslim. Both children are new to the school, and so have not been through the Foundation Stage in the English system. The class teacher is very positive and enthusiastic about having them as her pupils, but is having to work hard to find relevant background information and resources such as stories and information books from their home countries. She is a little wary of the anticipated requirements related to the children's Muslim identities but willing to find out and to be flexible in her teaching. She is very keen to establish good relationships with the children's families as she sees this as a support for her in meeting the needs of their children.

Activity 1.5
Understanding diversity

Each of the five children in the vignettes have particular experiences and knowledge that can be seen as strengths as they benefit their learning in mainstream school, and particular gaps in their experience that may create issues for their progress and their achievements. Make a chart like the one below and, in discussion with other trainees or colleagues in your placement school, list what you think could be seen as each child's strengths and needs, from the vignettes. There are some suggested answers at the end of the chapter on page 19.

child	strengths	needs
Yasmin		
Stefan		
Jan		
Umaru		
Radia		
Hamida		

3. Language diversity and learning – some myths and misconceptions

This brief, final section is intended to begin to raise some questions in your mind about the best approaches to teaching children with EAL. You may already have experience of teaching English to children or adults in other countries, which is normally defined as **English as a Foreign language (EFL)** teaching, and you may even have done a **Teaching English as a Foreign Language (TEFL)** course. There are parallels between EFL and EAL learners and some ideas from TEFL teaching can be very useful in EAL. But, there are also important differences, as the case studies in this chapter show. Some ideas from TEFL teaching may seem like common sense, but they can become myths and misconceptions when working with bilingual and EAL learners. They may not seem to be so helpful when you understand something of the complexities of the experiences of many bilingual and EAL learners. You will read a lot about theories of language, learning and bilingualism in Chapters 2 and 3, which will develop your understanding of the needs of bilingual and EAL learners. They will also help you to see how these myths and misconceptions can sometimes be unhelpful. So, here are my 'myths and misconceptions' – we will return to them at the end of the book, in Chapter 7.

- Languages should be kept separate in the classroom, or learners will become confused *(this is sometimes called 'language interference')*.

- Children will 'pick English up' naturally in the classroom; they do not need to be explicitly taught *(this is sometimes called 'immersion')*.

- Language diversity is a 'problem', and it is better if children speak English all the time in classrooms.

- It is impossible, or very difficult, to learn a new language beyond a young age *(this is sometimes called 'the critical period')*.

Learning Outcomes Review

This introductory chapter has provided you with background information about the children who are categorised as bilingual and EAL learners, and their families and communities. This should have helped you gain awareness of the history of language and cultural diversity in England, and the diverse range of experiences and knowledge that bilingual and EAL learners bring to their primary classrooms. One of the aims was to help you think about the importance of recognising and reflecting on your own views on language diversity and ethnicity for you as a primary teacher.

Self-assessment questions
1. In what ways do you think your own identity might influence your views and perceptions of the children you teach? Think about specific situations where this may have happened.

2. Why do you think it is important to understand something about the family backgrounds of the children you teach? (you will read more about this in Chapter 3).
3. Think about the teachers mentioned in each of the vignettes in this chapter. Following what you have read in this chapter, if you had been the teacher for any of the children described, would you have responded in the same way, or might you have done something different?
4. Think of a group of bilingual and EAL learners you know. Which of the categories introduced in section 1.2 would your learners fit into? Write a brief vignette of one of your learners, along the lines of those in the section.

child	strengths	needs
Suggested answers Activity 1:5 – understanding diversity		
Yasmin	• Strong speaking and listening skills • Supportive home and community • Diverse experiences of learning at home	• Sustained support in developing writing skills in English
Stefan	• Strong literacy in home language • Opportunities to develop expertise and take exams in home language	• Continued support in developing writing skills in English
Jan	• Teacher who is interested in understanding the problems he is facing • Positive attitude in class to recognising children's home languages	• Personalised provision to develop his skills in English
Umaru	• Good level of English language • Loving relationship with mother • Sympathy and caring environment in school	• Understanding (on the part of his teachers) of the broader cultural background of Sierra Leone • Personalised provision to help him catch up
Radia	• Supportive home and family background • Positive attitudes in school towards EAL children	• Improved communication between home and school
Hamida	• Supportive home and family background • Positive attitudes in school towards EAL children	• Greater awareness on the part of the school of cultural and religious factors underpinning Hamida's experiences

Further Reading

Gussin Paley, V. (2000) *White teacher*, 3rd edn. Cambridge: Harvard University Press.
This a personal account of teaching in a school which becomes increasingly diverse. Paley reflects on the way that even simple terminology can convey unintended meanings. She vividly describes what her pupils taught her over the years about herself as a 'white teacher'.

Hayes, D. (2011) Establishing your own teaching identity. In: Hansen, A. (ed) *Primary professional studies* (pp. 118–33). Exeter: Learning Matters.

This chapter encourages readers to think about their own values, motivation and self-identity, and the impact these have on becoming a teacher.

References

Arbeia Fort (2011) http://en.wikipedia.org/wiki/Arbeia (accessed 12 February 2012).

BBC (2007) *Multilingualism* www.bbc.co.uk/voices/yourvoice/multilingualism2.shtml (accessed 21 February 2012).

Datta, M. (2007) *Bilinguality and biliteracy: principles and practice,* 2nd edn. London: Continuum.

Department for Education (2011a) *Schools, children and their characteristics: January 2011* www.education.gov.uk/rsgateway/DB/SFR/s000925/index.shtml (accessed 12 February 2012).

Department for Education (2011b) *The National Strategies: New arrivals excellence programme: CPD modules* http://nsonline.org.uk/node/113690 (accessed 12 February 2012).

Hall, D., Griffiths, D., Haslam, L. and Wilkin, Y. (2001) *Assessing the needs of bilingual pupils: living in two languages,* 2nd edn. London: David Fulton.

Wikipedia (2011) *Languages of the United Kingdom* http://en.wikipedia.org/wiki/Languages_of_the_United_Kingdom (accessed 12 February 2012).

2. All about language

> ### Learning Outcomes
>
> ....
>
> This chapter will help you to achieve the following learning outcomes:
>
> - gain awareness and understanding of how language and learning can be theorised;
> - develop understanding of the functional approach to grammar and its importance for teaching and learning;
> - understand the important role of talk in children's learning in primary schools.

Introduction

Together with Chapter 3, this chapter introduces you to the theories related to language, learning and bilingualism that underpin the book. These will help you to understand the experiences of the bilingual and EAL learners you met in Chapter 1, and will meet in your own classrooms. The theories about language are relevant for your work with all primary children. They will help you to understand more about the role of language in learning generally and about the EAL learners you teach. They flow through the practical ideas presented in Chapters 4, 5 and 6 and will help you to make informed, practical decisions about the best ways to help your children to succeed.

There are questions and brief activities interspersed throughout the chapter to help you think about how the theories relate to your own experiences. Following Chapter 3, there is a set of 'key principles' to help you relate the theories to your teaching. Then, the principles are illustrated by practical examples in Chapters 4, 5 and 6. These will help you in planning and evaluating your own teaching strategies and resources for your bilingual and EAL learners.

These are the main sections and subsections of the chapter.

1. All about language
- What is language?
- Language, culture and identity
- Thinking about teaching languages – a functional approach

2. Language and learning
- Sociocultural theories of learning and the Zone of Proximal Development (ZPD)
- The importance of talk for learning

1. All about language

1.1 What is language?

Language pervades everything we do, at home and in our communities as well as at school and work. We experience language in an infinite range of ways through our everyday conversations with family, friends, colleagues and schoolmates. We use spoken language to engage in face-to-face conversations with the people near us. We communicate with those far away either through spoken language by phone or written language in a vast array of media, many of them online and **multi-modal**. Through language, we interact with others in the social groups we belong to, and construct our understandings of the world. This makes the learning of language in primary school, whether in literacy or modern foreign languages (MFL), very different from learning other subjects. It is cross-curricular in that it forms the basis of learning in all the other curriculum areas. For all primary children, and especially for EAL learners who are developing fluency in English, language learning takes place in every subject across the curriculum.

We all live in a multilingual society. It is important to remember that all the children you teach, not just those who are categorised as EAL or bilingual, have knowledge and experiences of languages and of varieties of English outside school that are different from those they use and learn in school. We are all continually exposed to different forms and varieties of the English language, and to different languages, in our everyday lives. We may hear and use different **dialects** of English, which have grammar and vocabulary different from **standard English**. We may speak English in different **accents** from the ones most commonly used in school and which are seen as appropriate for education. All of us, whether we regard ourselves as multilingual, bilingual or monolingual, have our own **repertoires,** or personal resources, of language. This means that we can choose different ways of speaking and writing in our interactions with others. We use our language repertoires to speak and write in different ways according to our audiences: our listeners and readers, making our choices according to the following factors, often called the '5Ws':

- *Who* we are speaking to or writing for (audiences);
- *When* and *where* (contexts);
- *What* we say or write (topics);
- *Why* we say or write these things (reasons and purposes).

For example, in an ordinary day, I may mumble a few words to my husband while eating breakfast, then set off down the road to the station, greeting our neighbour as he walks past with his dog. When I get to work, I head up the stairs to my office, switch on the computer, reply to several e-mails and compose a few of my own. After that, perhaps, I have to give a lecture to rows of students in a lecture theatre. This involves a very different way of speaking from the ones I have used so far – more like writing, in some ways. Later on, I may meet a smaller group of students in a classroom for a tutorial. Here, I need to use yet another way of speaking, one which is much more tentative and conversational. As I take part in the discussion, I need to listen carefully to my students' viewpoints and adapt the ways I speak in order to respond to their questions. On the way home from work, I may make a couple of quick calls on my mobile phone – yet another form of speaking, different from all the others I have already mentioned. In all of these interactions, I choose the ways I speak or write, depending on the '5Ws' indicated above – who, when, where, what and why.

Activity 2.1
Your language repertoire
Make a chart like the one below and list some of the ways you speak and write during a typical day. Answer the '5Ws' questions for each, following the examples given.

Activity	What	Who	When	Where	Why
Speaking	greetings	neighbour	early morning	in the street	to be friendly
Writing	e-mail	student	lunchtime	in the office	to answer a question

The notion of language repertoires is a very useful one in helping to understand how language works and in thinking about how your teaching can be made more focused and effective. It underpins what is known as the **functional approach** to language and grammar, which focuses on the purposes for which we need to use language, rather than just the language itself. If we help children to understand the functions – the '5Ws' – of the language in any task they are expected to do, then their thinking will be more focused and their language learning, through the activity, will be more meaningful, purposeful and successful. The functional approach to language is further explained in section 1.3.

1.2 Language, culture and identity

In addition to being an essential tool for learning, language is an inextricable part of our personal and social lives, of the cultures we live in, and of who we are. It is part of the way in which we develop a sense of where we belong, and how we fit in with the social worlds that surround us. In other words, it is part of our identities.

Research Focus

There is a great deal of evidence to show that, if children have a sense of belonging and of being valued in their classrooms, their attitudes to learning will be much more positive and their achievements will improve. Conteh (2003: 41–57) shows the range of knowledge and experiences that many bilingual and EAL learners bring to their mainstream classrooms, and suggests how it can support their learning in positive ways. On the other hand, children can very quickly gain the sense – even if

→

it is unintended – that their languages are not welcome and must be kept hidden from the teacher. This can have a negative effect on their learning, as the following example shows:

> Five-year old Rukshana began school speaking no English. Punjabi was the language of her home. Twenty years later, when she was training to be a teacher, she wrote about the way she felt as a child when, as a new child in the class, the teacher did not allow her to use Punjabi when assessing her knowledge of colours. This is part of what she wrote: 'The teacher left me staring blankly at the other children. Every one of them was doing something: playing, reading, working or talking in English. I sat back and felt sorry for myself the teacher was probably thinking 'just another incident with an Asian child who does not know colours' this was a day I felt so many emotions inside me. Feelings that I had never experienced before. I did not want to be myself.'

Bilingual and EAL learners need to feel that their home languages are recognised and valued in the classroom. To do this is often not difficult and it does not involve complex changes to the curriculum. Actions that may seem very small, such as doing the register in different languages or choosing a story with a particular setting or theme can make children feel recognised and valued, that they feel they belong in the classroom. This can open out their potential for learning, as the following case study shows.

Case Study: Valuing language diversity

A trainee teacher found out that there was a new child in her class who had recently arrived from an African country. She found out which country it was, and went to the library and chose a story to read to the class, which was set in the child's country of origin. It contained words in a language that neither the class teacher nor the trainee knew. She found out from the child's mother that they were greetings in one of the languages that the family spoke. With the trainee's (and her mother's) encouragement and support, the child taught the class how to say the greetings. The children enjoyed this very much. When the story was over, a little girl came up to the class teacher and the trainee and said, 'Miss, I can speak Arabic, and my dad teaches me every day. Shall I show you how to say hello?' The teacher was surprised, but pleased, and asked her to teach the class, which she did with a beaming smile on her face. The teacher told the trainee afterwards that the child had never done anything like that before. They concluded that she may have felt able to do so because of the positive 'space' that had been opened up for her by the story and the experience of learning greetings in a new language in the context of an enjoyable whole-class activity.

The links across identity, language and culture are strong. Languages are formed in the cultures in which they are situated, their meanings shaped through everyday use. The meanings of English words can change from country to country – light bulbs in Australia are called globes; roundabouts in west Africa are called turntables. Word meanings vary even in different parts of England. There is a story about some road signs put up about 30 years ago at level crossings in Lincolnshire and Norfolk, which read, 'Wait while lights are red'. Some drivers waited *until* the lights turned red, then tried to race across the track before the train thundered past! It quickly became clear that, in that part of the country, 'while' and 'until' had very similar meanings and the signs were rapidly changed. As teachers, we may sometimes need to think carefully about what our children are trying to say, and respond positively to their meanings, even though they may not always be expressed in terms that are familiar to us.

Children from Pakistani-heritage backgrounds, even when they are fluent in English, sometimes talk about their extended family members as 'brother cousins' and 'sister cousins'. When I first heard this, it reminded me of how people in Sierra Leone, where I had lived for several years, sometimes talked about their relatives. They would describe the relationships very precisely: 'he's my brother, same mother, same father' and so on. When I asked the Pakistani-heritage children why they talked about their cousins in this way, they told me that in Punjabi there were eight words for the one English word 'cousin'. So in their language, they could distinguish whether it was mum's sister's son, mum's brother's daughter and so on. I found this fascinating, and it led to several interesting discussions about families, comparing the different ways that we could think and talk about families in different cultures. This is an important way of learning (it certainly was for me), with clear links to personal and social education. It is also an excellent language learning activity.

It is very important for our self-confidence and identity as learners that we feel we belong and are valued in the communities in which we are learning. Bilingual children need to feel that their home languages are recognised in school, even if their teachers do not speak them. These languages are often a large part of their social lives outside school. Also, if they are in the early stages of learning English, the languages are a large part of their thought processes, as we will see in the discussion on bilingualism in Chapter 3. If you do not share your children's languages, you can still do a lot to show that you value them through using multilingual labels in the classroom, stories from their own cultures and dual language texts, of which there are now many. The dual language books website at the University of East London (UEL, 2011), which is discussed in Chapter 5, provides a lot of information. Resources such as these also help children to transfer their thinking from one language to another. Valuing children's out-of-school experiences and understandings in this way has been described as developing a **'funds of knowledge'** (Gonzalez et al. 2005) approach to their learning, and is discussed more fully in Chapter 3.

1.3 Thinking about teaching languages – a functional approach

Like any subject we are expected to teach, we need a way of thinking and talking about language in order to understand it ourselves and help children to learn it. Ways of describing languages are called **grammars,** and there are many different kinds. They are often not very helpful in teaching, as they can quickly become abstract and complex, the terminology difficult to remember and use. We often think of grammars as sets of rules to be followed, rather than ways of describing language. We can get very worried about what is 'correct', and anxious about making mistakes. A more useful way to think about grammar, perhaps, is what is known as the **functional** approach. This focuses on the choices we can make in using language to do the things we need to do. It is based on the idea, explained above, that in all the ways we use language to make meaning, we have choices – and we all have repertoires of language to choose from, whether we think of ourselves as bilingual or not. A functional approach encourages us to think about how we can say and write what we want to in the best ways possible, using the '5Ws' described above. Grammar can be thought of as a set of tools to help us do this. So, when thinking about language and how to teach it, the question of what is or isn't correct is not a very helpful one. Thinking differently about language and asking different questions, such as about whether the messages in the text have been conveyed in the best way possible, is often more productive. The answers to these questions will be different from text to text.

Activity 2.2

Saying things in the best way: Ted Hughes and *'The Iron Man'*

Look at the following text, which is from the beginning of *The Iron Man*, one of the best children's stories ever written (in my view!). Identify any features that may be described as 'incorrect' in the traditional way of thinking about grammar. Think about why Ted Hughes (who was poet laureate, so knew a thing or two about language) might have decided to open his story in this way. There are some suggestions to help you check your responses after this activity.

CRRRAAASSSSSSH

Down the cliff the Iron Man came toppling, head over heels.
CRASH!
CRASH!
CRASH!
From rock to rock, snag to snag, tumbling slowly. And as he crashed and crashed and crashed
His iron legs fell off.
His iron arms broke off and the hands broke off the arms.
His great iron ears fell off and his eyes fell out.
His great iron head fell off.

> *All the separate pieces tumbled, scattered, crashing, bumping, clanging, down on to the rocky beach far below.*
> *A few rocks tumbled with him.*
> *Then*
> *Silence.*
>
> Ted Hughes

These are some of the text features you might have noticed:

1. The use of capital letters and mis-spelt words – here they help you to imagine the Iron Man tumbling and crashing down the cliff.

2. There are lot of exclamation marks at one point – often they are thought to be 'bad' punctuation, but here they seem to help with describing the crashing of the Iron Man.

3. The sentence beginning 'From rock to rock…' is not really a sentence as it has no stated subject. But we all know that it is about the Iron Man, and it helps us, again, to imagine him rolling down the hill.

4. The next sentence begins with 'and'! but it fits in the overall description.

5. The section of the text beginning with 'His iron legs fell off…' is rather repetitive, with simple sentences, all with the same structure. But, again, it is effective as we imagine the pieces of the Iron Man falling off, one after the other.

6. There are no really descriptive adjectives ('wow' words) in the whole text, yet it is wonderfully descriptive. The most 'descriptive' words are the verbs.

Taking a functional approach means that we look at the ways in which language is used to construct **texts** in their **contexts of use,** rather than just the language itself. This means that, in their learning, children need to experience listening, speaking, reading and writing as authentic activities through which they can make meanings and do things, not just as a set of skills to be developed or lists of spellings to be learnt. In a functional approach to teaching, teachers explain and learners discuss the ways in which words are chosen and sentences are structured to construct whole texts such as stories, letters, reports and so on. All primary children – and particularly bilingual learners – need to experience examples of **authentic language** in their learning, not just made-up examples of language in tests, exercises, work sheets or traditional grammar books. They need to hear and read, think about, discuss and argue about real texts which writers have written for real purposes and audiences. To do this, they need to know about grammar. But the grammar will only make sense to them when they can relate it to real texts in this way.

Children learn much more effectively about how different texts work and are constructed if they have authentic purposes and audiences for their tasks. Rather than teaching text types in an abstract, mechanical way in literacy lessons, it is far more effective to introduce them through real tasks in different subjects across the curriculum. You can see some examples of this in

Chapter 4 in the discussion of planning. Then understanding of the text features can be reinforced and practised in literacy lessons with meaningful content that your children know something about. There are ideas to help you to do this, using activities across the curriculum, in Chapter 5.

Activity 2.3
Thinking about the functions of texts

All of the following are examples of authentic texts. Decide what kind of texts they are and where they come from (you could use the 5Ws questions to help you to do this). Then, think about what language features (grammar, punctuation, choice of words, etc.) the speakers or writers have used to make their texts meaningful and purposeful. There are some answers to these questions below.

1. 'Cheap day return to Manchester Piccadilly, please.'
2. To make wholemeal rolls, divide the dough into 18 equal portions. Each should weigh about 50g. On an unfloured surface, roll each piece of dough into a ball inside your cupped hand.
3. Parvana was small for her eleven years. As a small girl, she could usually get away with being outside without being questioned. 'I need this girl to help me walk,' her father would tell any talib who asked, pointing to his leg. He had lost the lower part of his leg when the high school he was teaching in was bombed. His insides had been hurt, somehow, too. He was often tired.
4. The Cold War is always portrayed as a global struggle between Communism and capitalism but in the early 1960s the world's Communist superpowers, China and Russia, also fell out. After a few border skirmishes they decided to continue their struggle in the rest of the world. So the Russia–China Cold War spread to Africa where they competed for allies.

---

1. This is a spoken text; the speaker wants to buy a rail ticket, they do not know the ticket seller personally, so they make their request in a very simple, straightforward way with no greetings or personal language. But, because the speaker is polite, they say 'please', because that is the way to express politeness in their culture (but not in all).

2. This is a written text, a recipe, in some ways similar to no. 1 in that it is giving instructions. So, it needs to be very clear to make sure that the reader has all the information they need to carry out the task. It uses 'bossy' or imperative verbs, and the writer has made sure that all the actions needed are placed in the correct order, and all measurements are accurate. The writer also uses some 'technical' language, e.g. 'on an unfloured surface' but illustrates what needs to be done by connecting with everyday, visual examples, e.g. '... roll into a ball inside your cupped hand'.

3. This is a written fiction text, a short extract from Deborah Ellis's book *Parvana's journey*, a fascinating children's novel about a young girl in Afghanistan during the rule of the Taliban,

which Ellis wrote after she had visited refugee camps and found out about the lives of women and children there. The short extract, from the beginning of the book, quickly sets the scene – why might Parvana be questioned if she is found outside? Why was her father's school bombed? Who did it? Who (or what) is a talib? What has happened to the rest of their family? The language is very simple, but we quickly gain an impression of the problems that Parvana faces.

4. This is a written non-fiction text, a short extract from Richard Dowden's book *Africa: Altered states, ordinary miracles,* published by Portobello Books in 2008. Richard Dowden is a journalist, so his style is straightforward, with the main facts presented at the start of the piece, and reasons and explanations coming later on. He uses a popular kind of 'personification' in the way he presents the 'struggle' between globalism and communism and China and Russia as 'falling out', like two people who have had a quarrel. This is a very vivid way of having the reader understand the events he is describing. If he was writing a history textbook, he would probably have used a more formal style, perhaps with longer, more complex sentences.

2. Language and learning

2.1 Sociocultural theories of learning and the Zone of Proximal Development (ZPD)

Research Focus

Learning is often described as 'sociocultural'. This suggests that learning is not simply the transmission of knowledge, but a process of negotiation and co-construction between teachers and learners. Vygotsky, one of the originators of sociocultural theories, through his research with children with special needs, argued that all learning is social in origin, and that young children develop and learn through 'externalised' social interactions with their teachers and their peers. As they grow, they develop the capacity to 'internalise' the interactions and to learn more independently. He used the idea of the **Zone of Proximal Development (ZPD)** to describe in a theoretical way this social mediation between teachers and children, suggesting that children learn interactively 'through problem solving under adult guidance or in collaboration with more capable peers.' (Vygotsky, 1978: 86).

The sociocultural theory of learning has very important implications for all children in primary classrooms, and particularly for bilingual and EAL learners. Sonia Nieto (1999) uses Vygotsky's theories to develop a model to describe the kinds of learning that will best support bilingual learners. She makes the point that it will promote learning for all children. Here are the four main elements in her model:

$\rightarrow$

- learning is actively constructed;
- learning grows from and builds on the learner's prior experiences;
- there are cultural differences in the ways that children learn;
- learning is socially mediated, and develops in cultural contexts .

One important conclusion we can draw from this is that while learning is something that we all do and so is a common human experience, the specific ways in which children learn will vary from individual to individual, depending on the knowledge and experiences they bring to the classroom. This is part of what Nieto means in her use of the word 'context'. In using the word, she is referring to more than just the learning environment in terms of the physical setting that surrounds the learners. Her concept of context includes all the social, cultural emotional, affective and cognitive resources – including languages – that both learners and teachers bring to the classroom setting. Other researchers besides Nieto argue that it also includes the political and historical influences reflected in the policies, resources and practices that make up the teaching and learning activities. As Nieto points out, this is a very empowering idea, as it means that every child is capable of learning. Most, if not all, children can learn successfully, given the teacher's understanding and mediation of all of these factors that influence their learning.

Bruner used Vygotsky's theories of learning to develop the notion of **scaffolding** for planning and teaching. His ideas are sometimes called 'a theory of instruction'. They are a way of thinking about how to develop teaching strategies to construct the best kinds of contexts to promote learning for individual children. To scaffold learning is more than providing 'support' – it is not just about helping children to do things, but helping them to do them independently. Beginning with context-embedded activities and gradually moving, with talk and action, towards less embedded activities means that children are never left without support. At the same time, they are encouraged to move forward to the new knowledge, which is the object of the activity. Scaffolding can be developed through a variety of practical resources and multi-sensory experiences, and there are many examples of these in Chapters 4 and 5.

2.2 The importance of talk for learning

Research Focus

There is a great deal of research that shows how collaborative classroom dialogues and discussions support cognitive development in individual learners. In *Constructing knowledge together*, Wells and Chang-Wells (1992) provide examples of talk from multilingual classrooms where children engage in 'collaborative sense-making' with their peers. Using Vygotsky's key concept of 'internalisation', they reveal how shared talk develops thinking. This could be seen in the way the

→

children could take part in discussions with each other, using much more complex language to consider and express their ideas than they would have been able to do on their own. The examples are similar to the discussions reported by Conteh (2003, 81–7), where children are negotiating how to carry out a 'fair test' in science to see which ball will bounce the highest. In the following example, Rehana, Yasmin and Nahida engage in collaborative talk about how to do the test, using language they probably would not be able to use on their own and co-constructing their understanding of what a fair test entails.

JC (teacher): . ... To answer the question, 'this is how I will make my test fair'.

Rehana: fair, I know how to make it fair

Teacher: yes

Rehana: with the ruler, if you hold it like that

Teacher: yes

Rehana: move it with your hand you've got to ... and I'll tell you something else, you've got to bounce it from the same height

Yasmin: do it from the same height

Nahida: same height

Teacher: why is it important to have a fair test?

Nahida: because like, if the other ball, and they bounce it in a different way, and then ... the other balls won't bounce like that, this way

As Wells and Chang-Wells argue, this kind of discussion is essential to help children to develop the thinking skills they need to become fully literate, and so become good readers and writers. Taking part in discussions, in any subject across the curriculum, is also one of the key means through which children become confident in using the academic language they need to develop the **cognitive academic language proficiency (CALP)** that is so essential for bilingual and EAL learners, and which is discussed in Chapter 3. In the *Expert Panel review of the National Curriculum* (DfE, 2011: 52–4), the importance of oral language across the curriculum is very clearly stated, in different ways:

> *whilst it should find a particular place within the National Curriculum for English, it should also be promoted more widely as an integral feature of all subjects.*

(page 53)

But literacy is, of course, the main route to academic success in our education system. Despite the fact that most of children's learning is mediated and accomplished in different ways through talk in the primary classroom, we need to remember that the evidence of their learning is usually contained in their writing, and they are almost always formally assessed through writing. It is essential that, as they move through primary school, talk needs to remains a central element of children's learning. Not only do they need to *learn to talk*, children also need to be able to *talk to learn*, across the whole curriculum. This has many implications for your planning, which are discussed in Chapter 4.

Activity 2.4

Talk for learning in the classroom

Using the '5Ws' again, make a chart and record all the examples you can think of across one day in your classroom where you think children were using talk for learning in any lesson. This will show you the range of ways in which your children are developing their talk repertoires.

Activity	What	Who	When	Where	Why
Mathematics mental starter	addition and subtraction up to 10	whole-class question and answer	start of lesson	on the carpet	to practise number bonds

Learning Outcomes Review

There are three learning outcomes for this chapter. They each focus on a particular theoretical aspect of language and learning, which is introduced in the chapter. The first is based on sociocultural theories and the notion of the ZPD; the second on functional grammar and the third on theories of learning and the role of talk in learning and literacy. Look back over these sections in the chapter, particularly the highlighted research focuses, and consider the following questions.

Self-assessment questions

1. What are some of the general implications of sociocultural theories of learning and the notion of the ZPD for organising and planning learning activities for primary children in general and bilingual and EAL learners in particular?
2. What are some of the differences between functional grammars and more conventional grammars?
3. In what ways do sociocultural theories of learning help us to understand the importance of oral language for learning in primary classrooms?
4. Why is it important to develop oral language across the curriculum? Look at the *National Curriculum Review* (2011) and follow up some of the references to talk across the curriculum.

Further Reading

Cummins, J. (2001) *Negotiating identities: education for empowerment in a diverse society*, 2nd edn. Ontario, CA, California Association for Bilingual Education.

This is perhaps the most comprehensive of Cummins' books. It explains in detail in a very readable way his ideas about the theories discussed in this chapter, and in the following chapter, and much more.

Thompson, G. (2004) *Introducing functional grammar*. London: Arnold.
Not for the fainthearted, but perhaps the most comprehensive and clearest account of functional grammar, for those who wish to gain understanding of its technical aspects. It provides exercises and activities to help develop your capacity to analyse texts using a functional approach.

References

Conteh, J. (2003) *Succeeding in diversity: culture, language and learning.* Stoke-on-Trent: Trentham Books.

DfE (2011) *The Framework for the National Curriculum: a report by the Expert Panel for the National Curriculum review.* London: Department of Education.

Gonzalez, N., Moll, L. and Amanti, C. (eds) (2005) *Funds of knowledge: theorizing practices in households, communities and classrooms.* New York: Routledge.

Nieto, S. (1999) *The light in their eyes: creating multicultural learning communities.* New York: Teachers College Press.

UEL (2011) *Using and researching dual language books for children* www.uel.ac.uk/duallanguagebooks/index.htm (accessed 12 February 2012).

Vygotsky, L. (1978) *Mind in society.* Cambridge: Harvard University Press.

Wells, G. and Chang-Wells, G.L. (1992) *Constructing knowledge together.* NH: Heinemann.

3. What does it mean to be bilingual?

Learning Outcomes

Learning Outcomes

This chapter will help you to achieve the following learning outcomes:

- develop understanding of what it means to be bilingual, and its implications for education;
- develop awareness of current research and debates about bilingualism in education;
- understand why it is important to recognise and value the experiences of learning that children have in their homes and communities.

Introduction

Together with Chapter 2, this chapter introduces you to the theories related to language, learning and bilingualism that underpin the book and help you to understand the experiences of primary children in general, as well as the bilingual and EAL learners you met in Chapter 1. They also flow through the practical ideas presented in Chapters 4, 5 and 6. The theories about bilingualism and education are based on extensive international research. They will help you to understand more about the bilingual and EAL learners you teach and to make informed decisions about the best ways to help all your pupils to succeed.

There are questions and brief activities interspersed through the chapter to help you think about how the theories relate to your own experiences, as well as their practical implications. Following this chapter, there is a set of 'key principles' for thinking about your planning and teaching. They will help you in planning and evaluating your own teaching strategies. These principles are illustrated by practical examples in Chapters 4, 5 and 6.

These are the main sections and subsections of the chapter.

1. What does it mean to be bilingual?
- The global context
- Being bilingual

2. Bilingualism in education
- Policy constructions: assessment and achievement
- Cummins' theories: CUP, language interdependence, BICS/CALP

3. The importance of learning outside school
- Home, family and community learning contexts – the 'funds of knowledge' concept

1. What does it mean to be bilingual?

1.1 The global context

English is the most widely used language in the world. It is spoken all over the world and around 80% of communication on the internet is in English, though other languages such as Mandarin are rapidly gaining ground (Center for Applied Linguistics, 1999). People all over the world are interested in learning English, advancing their study and working in English-speaking countries. About 25% of people in the world (and rising) speak English but those who speak it in addition to other languages outnumber those who speak only English by three to one. This means that about three-quarters of the conversations in English round the world are carried out by bilingual speakers. Around 80% of people in the world (and rising) are bilingual. So, for most people in the world, their normal everyday experiences are mediated in more than one language. Many more children are educated around the world in a second or additional language than in their mother tongue.

It is now generally accepted that being bilingual or multilingual brings benefits for educational success. Dutcher et al. (1994), in an extensive review of global research into multilingualism, drew some strong conclusions about the role of bilingualism in learning, which include the following.

- Development of the mother tongue needs to be encouraged to promote cognitive development and as a basis for learning the second language.
- Individuals most easily develop cognitive skills and master content material when they are taught in a familiar language.
- Individuals most easily develop literacy skills in a familiar language.
- Cognitive/academic language skills, once developed, transfer readily from one language to another.
- Success in school depends upon the child's mastery of cognitive/academic language, which is very different from the social language used at home.
- Parental and community support and involvement are essential.

These ideas have important practical implications for thinking about working with bilingual and EAL learners, and they link with Cummins' ideas, discussed in section 4.

1.2 Being bilingual

In Chapter 1, there is a full discussion about bilingual and **EAL** learners in England, and all the kinds of children who come under that category. When I use the term **bilingual** here, I include all those children who come under the 'EAL' umbrella, with their different language experiences and needs. I prefer the term 'bilingual' because I think it is broader and more inclusive than EAL. As we discussed in Chapter 1, for many bilingual pupils in England, English is not an additional language at all, but often their first and most dominant language. Using the term 'bilingual' also represents more accurately the important idea that, for such children, all their languages contribute to their knowledge of the world and their repertoires. It is important that teachers know about all the languages their pupils speak and write. Bilingual children and adults do not keep each language separate – they naturally switch and mix between the languages they have at their disposal. If you listen to groups of bilingual people talking to each other, you will often hear words, phrases or even sentences from English mixed with the languages they are speaking. This has been known as **codeswitching,** and is especially common in children whose families have been settled in the UK for two or three generations, and who still maintain strong links with their countries of origin.

Research Focus

A new term, **translanguaging,** is currently being introduced to replace codeswitching. Garcia (2009) suggests that it helps us think about a language identity which is 'brighter and more intense' than a monolingual one, and is a reflection of the wider choices available to bilinguals to make meaning. She argues that children (and adults) switch from one language to another in order to accomplish what they want to do, and to reflect their identities. They are not consciously thinking about which language to choose. The following example shows this. It was collected in a small study I conducted of how children made links between their learning in complementary and in mainstream settings. Sameena is an eight-year-old child, who is of third-generation Pakistani heritage. She was very proud that she gained level 3 in her KS1 maths SATs. Here she describes how she uses her knowledge of Punjabi to answer her class teacher's 'hot mental' questions at the start of the daily maths lesson. The children were asked to count in fives from 20 to 40:

> We had to count in fives, so I did it in my head in Punjabi then I said it out in English. Eek, do, teen, cha... twenty-five chey, saat, aat, nor... Thirty... Eek, do, teen, cha... thirty-five...

In trying to demonstrate how the counting in Punjabi is going on silently in her head while the performance of the English numbers is producing the correct answers, her voice varies. She almost whispers when she says the numbers in Punjabi and says those in English out aloud, repeating the counting from 1–4 and then from 6–9 in Punjabi and saying the relevant number in English in between. In this way, she accomplishes the task, in English, set by the teacher. Sameena is focused on answering her teacher's questions in order to affirm her identity as 'level 3' by showing she is good at mathematics. The language she needs comes naturally from her repertoire, which includes English and Punjabi numbers. Evidence like this makes us question the commonsense myth, mentioned in Chapter 1, that in learning a new language, you should not use the ones you already know as they might interfere.

Bilingual children in England often speak different languages with different family members as a perfectly normal part of their lives. They may speak English with their siblings, friends and perhaps their parents, but they will speak their home languages with uncles, aunts and grandparents. They will also, often, be learning the language of the religious books of their community and their **heritage languages** in a complementary class, which I discuss further in section 3. In a research project that was undertaken in Bradford in 2003, Aitsiselmi's study of languages used by people living in one area of Bradford (2004) revealed the complex ways in which members of different ethnic minority communities use all the languages and dialects in their repertoires. He notes the complications that some of his respondents faced when asked to name the languages they spoke. One simply said, 'we just call it apni zabaan' (our language).

Activity 3.1
Languages interview

Arrange to carry out an informal interview with a bilingual child or small group of children, in your class (or another class, if there are no bilingual learners in your own class). The aim is to find out about the languages they speak at home, how they use them, who they speak them with, what other learning experiences they may have, etc. Here are some suggested questions. Do not turn it into a formal interview – try to have a conversation with your informants.

1. Tell me about the languages you know.
2. Do you speak other languages with members of your family? Which ones?
3. Can you remember how you learned the languages you know?
4. Can you read any other language besides English?
5. Do you go to a Saturday class or a class outside school to learn other languages?
6. Do you go to any special clubs or places of worship where you speak other languages?
7. Do you have relatives in other countries who you speak different languages with, or write letters, emails, etc?
8. Can you teach me a little bit of your language?

In talking about bilingualism in this way, we are not suggesting that children are fluent in all the languages they speak and write, but that – like the majority of people in the world – they have access to more than one language in normal and natural ways in their daily lives. The following is a useful working definition of this kind of bilingualism. It is helpful in understanding the experiences of many bilingual and EAL pupils in schools in England. Hall et al. say that bilingual pupils are those who:

> ... live in two languages, who have access to, or need to use, two or more languages at home and at school. It does not mean that they have fluency in both languages or that they are competent and literate in both languages.

(p. 5)

This way of thinking about bilingualism makes clear the links between language and identity that were discussed in Chapter 2. An understanding and appreciation of these links is very important for success in education. Research into bilingualism and bilingual education by Cummins (2001) and many others resonates with the view of languages that Aitsiselmi discovered in his research in Bradford. It also challenges the myth, raised in Chapter 1, that when learning a second language, the learner's first language can 'interfere' and should be avoided.

As discussed in Chapter 1, in school, children can very quickly pick up messages about the languages they speak at home, even when they are unintended. They can feel that the languages have no place, and that being bilingual is not of any value. This, after all, reflects in many ways the prevailing attitude in the wider society. I once had a long and interesting conversation with a group of Year 6 children about their languages, the ways they used Urdu, Punjabi, English, French and Arabic and how their monolingual friends envied their knowledge. At the end, I asked them if they knew what the word **bilingual** meant. One boy responded, 'is it something to do with support?' It is essential that bilingual pupils recognise their own power, and the potential for learning that being bilingual gives them – and if they don't begin to do this in the primary school, it will be too late.

Underachievement at secondary school among minority ethnic pupils can be linked to the lack of support for their first languages as young learners, both in school and at home. This resonates with one of Nieto's key ideas about learning (see Chapter 2), that it grows from the cultural contexts in which the learner is situated. Instead of focusing on the 'problems' of having children who speak different languages in primary classrooms, it is much more positive to consider the possibilities that could open out if we see the children's languages as resources for their learning. As suggested in Chapter 4 in discussing groupwork in planning, research is beginning to show that bilingual learners in primary classrooms are eager to use their home languages for learning, and that this can have positive benefits across the curriculum, not just for learning English and for literacy.

2. Bilingualism in education

2.1 Policy constructions: assessment and achievement

> *No child should be expected to cast off the language and culture of the home as he* (sic.) *crosses the school threshold, nor to live and act as though school and home represent two totally separate and different cultures which have to be firmly kept apart.*

This much-quoted advice from the Bullock Report (DES, 1975: 286) is supported by what we know from research about the best ways to promote children's learning. We need to know about how children learn in different contexts, both in and out of school, and to use this knowledge to develop official policies and classroom practices which are truly inclusive. But, of course, to achieve inclusion through recognition and acceptance of diversity in this way is not easy.

The National Curriculum, first introduced in 1988, recognised above all that every pupil has an entitlement to learn English. Its key aim was that, by the age of sixteen, all pupils would be able to use spoken and written standard English confidently and accurately. Through all the years since its introduction, that aspiration has not changed. It has been described as a **monolingualising** curriculum, as no specific reference was made to children who may have two or more languages in their repertoires. There was no sense that, for such children, their entitlement to English might need to be effected in different ways from (so-called) 'monolingual' children. The National Curriculum Council did produce some guidance about language diversity (NCC, 1991) but it epitomised what Safford (2003: 8) calls 'the contradiction at the heart of education policy in England' for bilingual children. The circular welcomed language diversity as 'a rich resource', and went on to offer some guidance and support for teachers working with bilingual pupils. Essentially, it suggested that pupils be encouraged to use their first languages for learning only *until* their proficiency in English was strong enough for them to move to the exclusive use of English. Other languages were not seen as relevant to learning.

The outcome of these policy approaches has come to be known as **transitional bilingualism.** English and knowledge of English replace rather than grow from knowledge of other languages. Research has shown that transitional bilingualism can lead to restricted concept learning and problems with achievement. Instead of this, the theoretical and practical ideas in this book all promote a model of **additive bilingualism**. I believe that the best way to help bilingual pupils learn to their fullest capacity is to value their bilingualism, and to think of English as part of their ever-growing language repertoires, not as a replacement for their other languages. There is a great deal of research that supports this idea, such as the work of Cummins (2001), which is described in the next section.

When the National Literacy Strategy was introduced in 1998, there was still no recognition of the importance of bilingualism for learning. The first version of the *Framework for teaching* (DfEE, 1998) made no mention at all of bilingualism as a possible factor, either positive or negative, in learning to read and write. An additional section to the files was later distributed, which included provision for EAL learners, together with those with SEN and those in vertically grouped classes in small schools. Making such a link between SEN and EAL was unfortunate. It masked the fact that many EAL learners can have *language* needs rather than *learning* needs. It is no doubt true that they often need support, but this support can come from allowing them to use the languages they already know, rather than ignoring this knowledge. The same link between EAL and SEN was made in later versions of the National Curriculum, and has now become accepted, in some ways. Curriculum 2000 had an introductory statement about 'inclusion' (DfE, 2012) which talks about the 'potential barriers to learning and assessment' for pupils with SEN, disabilities and EAL.

Research Focus

Cummins (2001) argues, based on his research with French–English bilingual pupils in Canada, that the merging of bilingualism with special educational needs can have negative academic outcomes. It can lead to bilingual children being assessed as having learning needs and being placed in SEN groups, when in fact their needs are for specific language support in developing their competence in listening, speaking, reading and writing in order to cope with the demands of the curriculum. His theoretical models can help to understand the ways in which bilingual learners' experiences of language and learning need to be seen differently from those of children who do not 'live in more than one language'; some of his key ideas are explained in the next section.

Safford (2003: 8) suggests that we have 'two conflicting policy paradigms' in curriculum and assessment in England:

> ... the celebration of ethnic and linguistic diversity, and the universal model of language development and assessment.

For teachers working with bilingual children, assessment is a complex issue, as Safford shows in her account of following official requirements in trying to assess pupils from a wide range of language and cultural backgrounds. Many writers (e.g. Baker, 1996) spell out the negative implications for children's learning when assessment policies demand that we treat children as if they are all the same and expect them to attain the same targets in the same ways. Ultimately, this denies bilingual learners the means to develop to their full potential, and in effect, closes the door to educational success for them. Providing 'equal access' does not mean that we should treat all children in the same way. Doing this means that we often ignore some of the things that some children can do and the skills they have. We need to recognise the ways that national testing procedures do not give us a 'fair test' of all our children's full capabilities.

Imagine what the fish and the seal are thinking and feeling as they listen to what they have to do in the so-called 'fair' test in Figure 3.1 opposite! Can you also think about what skills and expertise they have, which they cannot use in climbing a tree? These skills are ignored in the 'universal' test.

Since 2002, the KS2 *Framework for Languages* (DfES, 2002) has brought new ways of thinking about language to the attention of primary teachers. This is the policy document underpinning the introduction of modern foreign languages (MFL) into primary schools. The aims of primary MFL (PMFL) teaching are very different from those of traditional secondary MFL teaching. Rather than seeking to develop proficiency in a specific language, PMFL is much more about building generic strategies for language learning and the positive values, attitudes and awareness that learning languages provides. The framework has two 'cross-cutting strands', *Knowledge about language* (KAL) and *Language learning strategies* (LLS). These are intended to stimulate children's creativity and ensure an international dimension in learning across the

Figure 3.1 An inclusive approach to assessment?

curriculum. Different languages can even be used for different learning intentions across the strands.

The objectives in the two strands lend themselves to a wide range of activities that, besides promoting children's learning of different languages, can get them exploring their local communities and their wider society as they develop global awareness and understanding. They can be met in ways that include families and affirm their funds of knowledge as well as those of bilingual staff in the school. These kinds of activities promote the best kinds of learning for bilingual pupils, and examples of these can be found throughout Chapters 4 and 5.

Activity 3.2
KS2 Framework for languages: making links

Get hold of a copy of the *KS2 Framework for languages* – it is online, if you cannot find a hard copy. Read the guidance on page 11 about the structure of the framework, in particular the information about the *Knowledge about language* (KAL) and the *Language learning strategies* (LLS). Then, look at the KAL and LLS objectives for one of the years (it doesn't matter which, but you could do this with colleagues and each focus on a particular year, then share your findings). Think about how they link with children's learning of literacy, and what activities you might do, to help your children achieve them.

2.2 Cummins' theories

Research Focus

Cummins' ideas are well known throughout the world, and provide powerful explanations for many distinctive features of bilingualism. They show how the learning of first and additional languages are always linked, and how academic language proficiency needs time to develop. The key difference in Cummins' thinking and writing from many other writers about second language acquisition is that he includes learners' first languages in the second language acquisition process. This is why his work is more relevant for understanding the needs of bilingual learners in England than models taken from other 'theories' of language learning such as **Second Language Acquisition (SLA)** and **English Language Teaching (ELT)**. I will discuss three of his main ideas that are very relevant to understanding the needs of bilingual and EAL learners in primary schools; the first two, *Common underlying proficiency (CUP)* and *linguistic interdependence*, are helpful in understanding the ways that bilingual learners process and use their languages and the third, *BICS/CALP*, is a way of thinking about the kinds of language that successful learners need to know.

CUP and linguistic interdependence: It used to be believed that a bilingual person had two or more language systems at their disposal, and that moving between the two could be confusing. So, in teaching, it was thought that the languages had to be kept separate in order to avoid the first language 'interfering' with the new language being taught. Cummins observed the ways that bilingual children used their languages both in oracy and literacy. He recognised that languages were not kept separate, but that bilinguals switched between their languages in ways such as those described in section 1.2 above. So, he concluded that instead of a separate proficiency for each language that they could speak, read or write, all human beings have some kind of common underlying proficiency (CUP) for language. This could be imagined as a sort of reservoir of language understanding, knowledge and skill, which is drawn on to make the meanings that the language user needs in the context in which they are situated. This clearly links with the ideas about language repertoires and choices that I discussed in Chapter 2.

Cummins' famous 'iceberg' diagram represents the CUP. My version is in Figure 3.2. The horizontal line is the boundary between the language user's inner capacity in their brain, and the outside world. The tips of the iceberg represent the languages being used, whether it is L1, L2 or any further languages. These draw on the part of the CUP iceberg which is hidden, but which supports all the language choices that the user makes.

The idea of the CUP clearly links with the notion of language repertoires. It also underpins the theory of linguistic interdependence, which Cummins describes as follows.

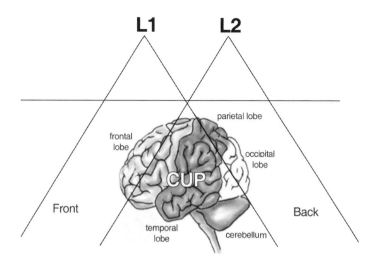

Figure 3.2 Cummins' iceberg diagram of the CUP

Knowledge and understanding of one language links to knowledge and understanding of new languages – this is especially significant in relation to literacy.

The following case study, of a nine-year-old 'new arrival', provides compelling evidence of the ways that literacy in his first language opened up his learning of English.

Case Study: Making links

Mushtaq was nine years old when he arrived from Bangladesh, unable to speak any English at all. On his first day in school, he was sent to join my 'language support' group where we were doing some story-based activities. He spent the whole lesson in silence while the rest of the group worked on an African story about the sun and moon. The next day, Mushtaq gave me a piece of paper covered in a neatly written script. I did not know what the script was, and was amazed when I discovered it was the sun and moon story, written out in Bengali. His classmate had re-told him the story and he had written it out for me. So it turned out that Mushtaq was already highly literate in Bengali. The following week, he contributed to a trilingual book that we made about the story. The writing in the top right-hand corner of the page is his (see Figure 3.3).

Over the next few weeks, Mushtaq contributed to several other trilingual books like this, and also made some story tapes where he read stories in Bengali for other children to listen to. Within six months, he was one of the best readers in his class – in English.

Once again, the key message here is that we must find out about the languages that our children can speak, read and write outside the mainstream classroom. It does not matter if we cannot speak, read or write them ourselves – I cannot speak Bengali, and did not even know what language it was when I first saw the script on Mushtaq's paper. We must value the

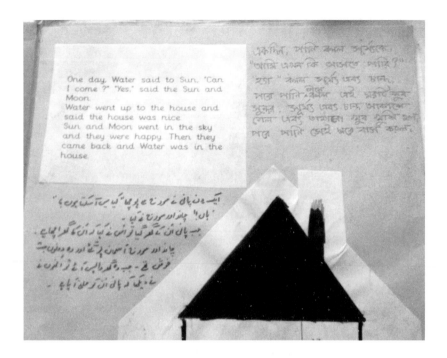

Figure 3.3 Children's trilingual book

knowledge that our pupils bring to the classroom and help them find spaces in which they can construct their own ways of learning, beginning from what they already know.

BICS (Basic Interpersonal Communication 'Skills')/CALP (Cognitive Academic Language Proficiency)

These well-known, but sometimes misunderstood, acronyms underpin an important idea that Cummins has developed over the years about the ways languages are learnt. It has relevance for all pupils, but is of particular relevance for bilingual and EAL learners. BICS/CALP are sometimes described as 'skills' or even specific features of language to be taught and tested, but this does not really reflect what they are. It is sometimes said that BICS is more to do with spoken language and CALP with written, but again this is not really what Cummins meant.

Basically, BICS refers to all the social, everyday things we do with language, embedded in familiar contexts, such as greetings, conversations, retelling, describing, recalling, and so on. CALP, on the other hand, refers to all the, usually more cognitively demanding, things we need to do with language in order to achieve academic purposes, such as explaining, analysing, arguing, and so on. BICS relates to the kinds of language which develop first, usually in face-to-face, highly contextualised situations. CALP develops through engaging in more decontextualised situations and discussions, and so is often seen as more complex. CALP has two main dimensions: it is the **cognitive language** with which we can think and do demanding things, such as investigating, exploring ideas, analysing, hypothesising and solving problems. It is also the kind of **academic language** that we find in textbooks, lecture notes and so on. This often has features such as the passive voice, vocabulary with Greek and Latin roots, the use of metaphor and personification and the use of abstract nouns, such as *information* from *inform* and *hunger* from *hungry*.

Cummins has developed the notions of BICS and CALP over the years, and he now writes of them as a continuum, rather than two separate aspects of language. Educated adults move back and forth across the continuum according to the demands of their language interactions, and we should be aiming to develop this capacity and confidence in the children we teach. The BICS/CALP model is relevant for all children – all children need opportunities to use a wide range of language and languages in different ways in their learning. The model also has implications which are specific to bilingual learners. Cummins found that children entering school with very little English would develop BICS (i.e. fluency in the kinds of language interactions suggested above) quite quickly, usually within 18 months to two years. But full capacity in CALP would take a lot longer. Cummins concluded that this could take at least seven years. It is also clear that the progression from BICS to CALP is not automatic, and that children need to be supported as they move from learning through context-embedded activities to the more disembedded tasks they are expected to perform as they move up the primary school. In this process, it is crucial that bilingual learners have continued access to their first languages for their learning.

The BICS/CALP ideas can help us to see through the confusion between language needs and learning needs that I talked about in section 2.1. Children enter school unable to speak English and at first, they can seem to do very well. They learn to do all the social things they want to do with language, and everything seems very promising. Then, things slow down as the long slog to develop CALP begins. Sometimes, children do not seem to make progress at all. This is because their thought processes are still largely in their first language, and they are – literally – learning to think in a new language. Unfortunately, it is at this point, usually, that the assessment wheel starts turning and children find themselves placed in SEN groups and even diagnosed with learning difficulties. Often, all they need is time and the opportunity to continue using their first language to support their thinking in the new language.

3. The importance of learning outside school

3.1 Home, family and community learning contexts – the 'funds of knowledge' concept

As I explained in Chapter 1, it is important to remember that, for many bilingual learners, formal learning does not end when they go home from their mainstream school in the afternoon. Many attend community-based schools in mosques, synagogues, churches, temples, and other complementary classes. They learn to read and write their heritage languages and the languages of their religions. Many students go on to take GCSE and A-level exams in Urdu, Gujerati, Bangla, Polish, Chinese and other languages. There is a growing body of research into the ways that children learn in their complementary classes, and the links that they can make between their complementary and mainstream learning, such as Sameena in the example in section 1.2 of this chapter.

Many bilingual pupils experience learning in different contexts, but often, their teachers in one system know very little about what goes on in the other. There is no link between their different learning contexts, and children are left to make their own sense of the learning demands on them. One Year 6 boy, whom I interviewed as part of a small research project, talked about his learning in the mosque in a very insightful way, describing the different things his teachers did in his mosque school and his mainstream school. He ended with a very powerful and deeply felt comment:

> *I think the mosque and school should be together . . . it's like the same thing . . . you're teaching something, you're getting knowledge from people . . .*

As well as finding out about the languages that the pupils in your class speak, it is very worthwhile to find out about the different schools they attend, and what they are learning there. This will make them feel that you are interested in them and value them as individuals. It will also increase your knowledge of your pupils' home and community experiences.

Activity 3.3
Learning in home and community
In a school with EAL learners, find out what the policies are for working with parents and families to support their children's learning. Think about how they might help to access family 'funds of knowledge'.

Find out if the school has a home–school liaison officer (HSLO) and ask if you can talk to them about what they do, and how they work to develop links between home and community and school. If you can, try to visit a community or complementary school.

We also need to be aware of the ways that children are learning in the home, and of how this contributes to the 'funds of knowledge' that they bring to their learning in more formal, mainstream settings. Children are often involved in interpreting and translating for family members who may have very limited English; they take part in extended family activities such as weddings and celebrations for Eid and other religious events. They sometimes travel to their countries of origin or to visit relatives in other parts of the world. All of these experiences offer possibilities for learning, with the added benefit of affirming the children's identities as members of dynamic, diverse communities. Families mediate every child's first learning experiences, and it is the responsibility of the school to build on this in whatever ways it can. Ideas for this, related to learning across the curriculum, are provided in Chapters 4 and 5.

Learning Outcomes Review

The three learning outcomes for this chapter are all to do with understanding the language and cultural experiences of the bilingual and EAL learners you will be teaching. Here are some questions to consider in thinking about these outcomes.

Self-assessment questions

1. How have your views about bilingualism and bilingual learners been changed by the ideas you have read about in this chapter?
2. How do your personal experiences of language diversity and bilingualism compare with the ideas you have read about in this chapter?
3. In what ways could we assess bilingual and EAL learners' learning without depending on their capacities in English? Can you think about how you could do this with children that you teach?

Further Reading

Conteh, J. (2003) *Succeeding in diversity: culture, language and learning in primary classrooms.* Stoke-on-Trent: Trentham Books.

Based on research with successful bilingual KS2 learners and their families, this book develops many of the ideas discussed in this chapter and includes evidence from interviews with families and teachers and classroom observations to illustrate the arguments developed.

Hall D., Griffiths D., Haslam L. and Wilkin Y. (2001) *Assessing the needs of bilingual pupils: living in two languages*, 2nd edn. London: Fulton Books.

A clear, practical and concise account of the tensions between 'EAL' and 'SEN', with useful guidance for planning. This will help you ensure that the language and cognitive demands of your activities provide support and progression for bilingual learners.

References

Aitsiselmi, F. (2004) *Linguistic diversity and the use of English in the home environment: a Bradford case study.* Department of Languages and European Studies, School of Social and International Studies, University of Bradford.

Baker, C. (1996) *Foundations of bilingual education and bilingualism*, 2nd edn. Clevedon: Multilingual Matters.

Center for Applied Linguistics, Washington, DC (1999) *A global perspective on bilingualism and bilingual education* (Online resources: digests) www.cal.org/resources/Digest/digestglobal.html (accessed 21 February 2012).

Cummins, J. (2001) *Negotiating identities: education for empowerment in a diverse society*, 2nd edn. Ontario, CA: California Association for Bilingual Education.

Department of Education and Science (DES) (1975) *A language for life* (The Bullock Report). London: HMSO.

Department for Education and Employment (DfEE) (1998) *The National Literacy Strategy: Framework for Teaching.* London: DfEE.

Department for Education and Science DfES (2002) *Key Stage 2 framework for languages, parts 1, 2 and 3* http://nationalstrategies.standards.dcsf.gov.uk/node/85274 (accessed February 21, 2012).

Department for Education (DfE)(2012) *Including all learners* www.education.gov.uk/schools/ teachingandlearning/curriculum/b00199686/inclusion (accessed 21 February 2012).

Dutcher, N., in collaboration with Tucker, G.R. (1994) *The use of first and second languages in education: a review of educational experience.* Washington, DC: World Bank, East Asia and the Pacific Region, Country Department III.

Garcia, O. (2009) *Bilingual education in the 21ˢᵗ century: a global perspective.* Wiley-Blackwell.

National Curriculum Council (NCC) (1991) *Linguistic diversity and the National Curriculum,* circular number 11 (York: National Curriculum Council).

Safford K. (2003) *Teachers and pupils in the big picture: seeing real children in routinised assessment.* Watford: National Association for Language Development in the Curriculum (NALDIC).

Principles for planning for bilingual learners

These six key principles for planning lessons and activities for bilingual learners have been developed from the ideas discussed in Chapters 1 to 3. In Chapters 4 to 6, I will use these principles to present practical examples of activities and strategies to promote bilingual children's learning in speaking and listening, reading and writing across the curriculum.

1. Developing a positive ethos that reflects language and cultural diversity at whole-school level supports home-school links, and encourages families and schools to work in partnership.

2. In the classroom, providing opportunities for bilingual pupils to use their first languages in everyday activities opens out potential for learning and affirms their identities.

3. Pupils need every possible opportunity to explore ideas and concepts orally in all subjects across the curriculum.

4. Before beginning extended writing activities, pupils need plenty of chances for collaborative discussion and practical experience.

5. Promoting awareness of language systems and structures by allowing bilingual pupils to analyse and compare the different ways of saying things in the languages they know helps develop their CALP and also promotes language awareness among their monolingual classmates.

6. Providing extensive opportunities for hands-on experience enhances language learning and learning more generally.

PART 2
PROMOTING LEARNING – PRACTICAL APPROACHES FOR BILINGUAL AND EAL LEARNERS

4. Planning across the curriculum for bilingual and EAL learners

Learning Outcomes

This chapter will help you to achieve the following learning outcomes:

- develop understanding of how to plan to promote learning across the curriculum that links with pupils' home and community experiences;
- develop awareness of different ways to plan and organise group work to promote learning for bilingual and EAL learners;
- gain greater understanding of the importance of speaking and listening for children's learning generally and for bilingual and EAL learners in particular.

Introduction

All of the ideas presented here build on the theories about language and learning that are introduced in Chapters 2 and 3. The learning outcomes for the chapter are interlinked with the six principles for planning at the end of Part 1. In this way, you can see how oral language is a central factor in learning, and how you can build it in to your planning for all subjects across the curriculum. This, of course, is important for all children in primary school, not just bilingual and EAL learners.

Interspersed through the sections of this chapter, there are questions and activities to help you to think further about the ideas that you are reading about as well as to think practically about your planning in all subjects across the primary curriculum in your classroom. There are some suggestions for further reading at the end of the chapter.

These are the sections and subsections of this chapter:

1. Planning across the curriculum
- Starting points – developing plans
- The Cummins' quadrant

2. Organising classes and groups for learning
- Planning for collaborative talk
- Including new arrivals in your lessons – buddies and mentors
- Planning for using home languages in learning

1. Planning across the curriculum

1.1 Starting points – developing plans

Developing medium-term and short-term plans to promote the learning of bilingual and EAL children is complex. But do not be tempted simply to follow plans you find on the internet or in published schemes of work. Spend time thinking carefully about and constructing your own planning, and you will understand much more fully what you are proposing to teach, and why. This will pay off in the quality of your lessons as well as in the learning and behaviour of your children. You will also build up a stock of ideas and strategies that you will be able to use over and over again.

For children who are at the early stages of developing English, there are always two strands involved in their learning. They need to learn:

● the curriculum content;

and they also need to learn to use...

● the English language in increasingly academic ways in order to access the curriculum.

Of course, this is true for all children, but it is clearly more important for many EAL learners who often need to catch up with their peers in terms of their knowledge of English. Maggie Gravelle (1996) explains this point thus:

> *Bilingual learners need both the curriculum that motivates and has relevance for them and the systematic language development and feedback that enables them to achieve within it.*

At the same time, it can be the case that some bilingual learners will be ahead of some of their classmates in their understanding of the concepts and content in some curriculum subjects, but they may not have the English vocabulary and grammar to show you what they know. This is often the case with mathematics. Children who are relatively new to English can find it quite frustrating if they are given tasks to do that are far below their academic capability in a subject. It is very important that you find out whether your 'new to English' children have been to school in their countries of origin, and try to get some idea of what they may have learnt. Secondly, you need to think about teaching the curriculum content in interesting and challenging ways, alongside making sure you accommodate the time that is necessary to teach the specific English language that your pupils need to access and express their understanding of that content.

The functional way of understanding language and grammar will help you to clarify the language demands of the subjects you are teaching. It reminds us that we need to be clear about two important language-related elements in planning, which are:

● what we are expecting our pupils to be able to *do* with the language they are learning;

● the *kinds* of language they will need to do these things.

In order to do this, we need to go beyond thinking about just the key vocabulary that our children may need in order to learn concepts and content in different subjects across the curriculum. We also need to think about how to help them become familiar with the ways the language is organised grammatically and textually – in other words, the kinds of spoken and written texts they will be using and constructing in their learning. For example, in science, they will no doubt be following instructions – as well as making up their own – and perhaps writing reports; in history and other humanities subjects, they will be taking part in discussions and debates, and so on.

Remember that texts are spoken as well as written. We now feel very familiar in literacy with the idea of teaching the different text types children need to know for their writing, but the suggestion that we can also teach them the different ways in which they need to use language in speaking is a fairly new one. This will be discussed further when we introduce the Cummins' quadrant in the following section.

Activity 4.1

Text types for learning

Make a table like the one below showing the main text types that pupils are expected to learn about in literacy. In the second column, list the subject areas for which you think each text type is relevant. Remember that the text types can apply to different subjects. In the third column, list some of the different kinds of texts that you think children need to be able to learn and use in different subjects across the curriculum. Include spoken as well as written texts. There are some examples to start you off.

Text type	Curriculum area	Example of text
Reports	science, history	A written report of a 'fair test' that the children have conducted. Warriors reporting to their chief what happened in a Viking raid on a Northumbrian village (role play).
Discussion texts		
Reference texts (explanations)	geography	A weather forecast as part of a radio or TV programme.
Persuasive texts		
Recount		
Instructions		

Relating different text types to areas of the curriculum in this way helps us to think about the language demands of all the different subject areas and of the particular tasks we are asking our pupils to do. If we combine this with the first principle for planning and identify ways in which we can make the curriculum content build on the prior experiences of our learners, this will help in working out how to make the content and the language of the tasks we plan more interesting and relevant for bilingual and EAL pupils – indeed for all pupils. There are ideas in Chapter 5 for strategies and resources that help you to do this.

An excellent way to begin planning a topic or a new area of the curriculum is to make a **KWHL** grid. This is a variation on the well-known **KWL grid**. It encourages you to ask four rather than three questions about the new area for learning, in order to help you to clarify the main elements to be included in your planning, as well as begin to think about how you might teach it.

- What do my pupils already *know*?
- What do I *want* them to find out? (check the curriculum)
- *How* will they find this out?
- What will they *learn*?

Figure 4.1 depicts a KWHL grid, which a trainee teacher made to begin planning for his Year 3 class to do a science-based topic about the life cycles of plants and animals. Notice how he included in the first column both the content knowledge and the language knowledge from different areas of the curriculum that he knew his children had done and so would be able to bring to their new topic.

What we know (K)	What we want to find out (W)	How we will find this out (H)	What we will learn (L)
The hungry caterpillar story Words to describe family members: mum, dad, grandma, brother, baby, sister, etc Names for animals and their babies: sheep/lamb; dog/puppy; cat/kitten How to write instructions	Life cycle of butterflies and moths Different parts of a plant Stages of development in plants Stages of development in animals Life cycles of different kinds of animals	Plant seeds in the classroom and observe them growing Look carefully at plants and compare to illustrations in books or on the internet Use information books to find out about animals in other countries Outing to Butterfly World	How to draw butterflies, plants and animals How to read carefully to find out specific information How to put pictures, words and sentences in the correct order to provide information

Figure 4.1 A KWHL grid

When you complete the first column, spend a bit of time thinking about both the language and the content knowledge that the children already have. This will help you to generate a bank of both content ideas and language for planning your activities. The next step is to think about how to sequence the activities to develop appropriate progression in your planning. The Cummins' quadrant is very helpful for this.

1.2 The Cummins' quadrant

Cummins' ideas about the common underlying proficiency (CUP), basic interpersonal communication 'skills' (BICS) and cognitive academic language proficiency (CALP) are explained in Chapter 3. They are very helpful when we come to think about planning. They help us to think about how to structure activities and sequences of activities to promote learning for our children in three dimensions, namely:

• conceptual development;

• language development;

• progression in learning.

At the same time, Cummins' ideas about the CUP help us to understand how *all* the knowledge of any languages that children bring to their classrooms can be seen as a resource to support their learning of any subject. We need to find ways to tap into the full repertoire of our pupils' language resources. The following sections, on classroom organisation and using pupils' home languages, have some ideas to help with this.

The BICS and CALP concepts have many implications for medium-term planning and also for lesson planning. We need to think about how to structure and sequence activities in order to support children's progress in their learning from context-based, cognitively less demanding activities that mainly use informal language (BICS) to the more academic and cognitively demanding tasks that require more academic language (CALP). In planning, we need to start with activities at the level where pupils can use their BICS-related language skills, and gradually move into activities which are more demanding cognitively and where CALP-related language capacity and knowledge come into play. In this way, we will be scaffolding pupils' academic learning and providing the means for them to develop deep and rich conceptual understanding of the subjects they are learning. At the same time, we will be providing increasingly demanding and language-rich activities that will scaffold pupils' learning of English and enhance their confidence as speakers and writers of English in a wide range of ways.

Cummins developed a quadrant framework to show how BICS and CALP could be developed through planning and teaching (Figure 4.2). It is helpful in identifying, developing and sequencing appropriate tasks in different curriculum areas for all pupils, and especially so for bilingual learners.

The two axes can be thought of as continua, with contextual support on the horizontal axis and cognitive demand on the vertical. The horizontal axis, moving from left to right, encourages you to think about progressing from context-embedded learning to that which is much less dependent on the immediate context. The vertical axis relates to the degree of cognitive demand and involvement in a task, which clearly relates to the language demands. It moves upwards, from tasks that are not very demanding to increasingly challenging activities.

Good planning for concept learning and language development will ensure that pupils always move from activities with a high degree of contextual support, such as real objects, pictures,

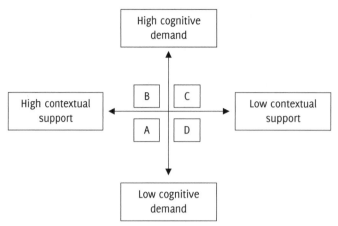

Figure 4.2 The Cummins' quadrant

hands-on activities and so on, to those which are less contextually supported in these ways. At this higher level, activities will be much more dependent on the linguistic cues and the pupils' own knowledge of language, as well as what they have already learnt. The following case study, in mathematics, shows how your activities could progress through the quadrants.

Case Study: Progression in mathematics in Reception

If you are teaching children in Reception or Year 1 about the properties of different shapes, the progression from activities with low cognitive demand and high contextual support to activities with high cognitive demand and low contextual support might look something like the following.

- Quadrant A: activities which involve pupils in touching and handling plastic shapes, talking about them, making patterns and pictures with them, describing, matching and beginning to compare them.

- Quadrant B: activities which move pupils to seeing and talking about the shapes as visual representations, such as matching shapes to pictures, finding objects in the classroom which are particular shapes, talking about what is the same, similar or different about a collection of shapes or pictures.

- Quadrant C: activities which encourage pupils to think and talk (and perhaps write and draw) about the shapes without immediate visual or concrete support, such as answering questions (or making up their own questions) about a square and how it is different from a triangle, making a chart about the similarities and differences of shapes, drawing shapes following instructions given by the teacher or other adult, or their peers.

- Quadrant D: There should be no acitivities in this quadrant as they would not promote the children's learning.

In Conteh, 2006 (p.11), I described this progression through the three quadrants in Cummins' diagram like this:

> *Beginning with context-embedded activities and gradually moving, with talk and action, towards less embedded activities means that children are never left without support, and at the same time are being encouraged to move to the new knowledge which is the object of the activity.*

The kinds of activities that fit into each quadrant, defined by their conceptual and language demands, are categorised in Figure 4.3.

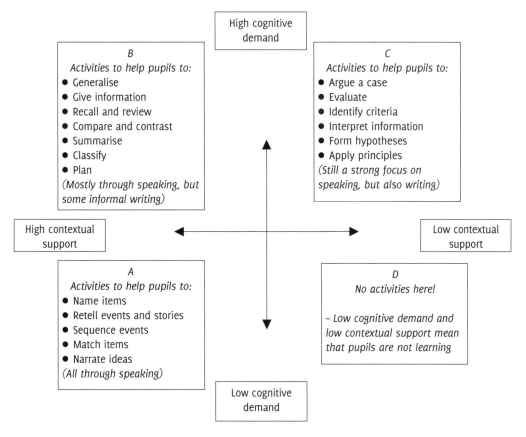

Figure 4.3 Planning for learning using the Cummins' quadrant

The role of oral language is clearly important for activities in quadrant A, but it is not the case that speaking and listening become less important as we move to activities in quadrants B and C. At all stages, talk remains a key vehicle for learning. It is vital that you plan activities which provide opportunities for pupils to use talk in more sophisticated and adventurous ways, at the same time as supporting them in trying out ways of speaking which may not be familiar to them. This helps them to develop confidence as speakers of English and to think about and learn the new concepts in the subject you are teaching. Pauline Gibbons (1998) talks about the 'teacher-guided reporting' stage of the activity, which equates to quadrant C. Wells and Chang-

Wells (1992) discuss the 'three modes of interaction' which pupils need to develop through talk, and which they regard as essential for learning. They can also be seen as corresponding to Cummins' quadrants A, B and C.

A: Shared understanding.

B: Expert guidance.

C: Reflection.

It is at the reflection stage that children are talking in much more formal, discursive and analytic ways. Their understanding of the content is being enhanced and they are also using the language they will need in their writing.

Let us think about planning a set of story-based activities in literacy. The overall aim (or key learning objective) of the activities may be to have pupils write their own version of a story or write from a particular character's viewpoint. A sequence of activities based on the story that helps pupils to progress through quadrants A, B and C might look something like Figure 4.4. The children may not actually get down to any formal writing at all in the first three or four lessons, but when they do come to the task of writing, they will have a rich stock of words, structures, ideas and understanding of the story to bring to it.

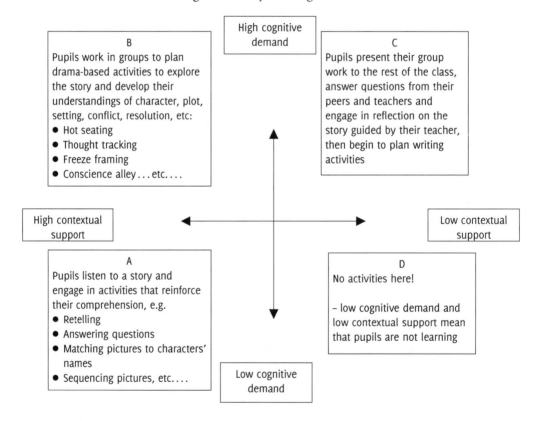

Figure 4.4 Cummins' quadrant and literacy planning

Hall et al. (2001) have some examples of Cummins' quadrants which show the progression of activities in science and there are examples of planning for mathematics using the quadrant diagram on the NALDIC website (NALDIC, 2011).

> ## Activity 4.2
> **Planning for progression**
> Using the Cummins' quadrant and the ideas and diagrams above, look at some of your planning in a particular area of the curriculum. See if you can identify which activities might fit into each of the four quadrants, and consider whether you could re-order the activities to build in better progression or whether you need more activities in any quadrant.

A key point that emerges from thinking about planning in this way is that, alongside planning the content and progression of the teaching activities, we need to think carefully about ways of organising classes and groups of pupils to facilitate their learning, and this is the focus of the following section.

2. Organising classes and groups for learning

2.1 Planning for collaborative talk

If you want to provide as many opportunities as possible to promote talk for learning, you need to have flexibility in organising both the classroom space and the seating and positioning of your pupils. In this section, we will consider ways of grouping pupils for talk. Simply placing pupils in groups around tables does not mean that they will engage in learning through talk. Your activities need to be structured so that you progressively build your pupils' understandings of the content and concepts they are learning. The kinds of talk that your pupils need to do should become increasingly complex as they move through the activities. They should be expected and able to talk in increasingly well-informed, thoughtful and independent ways about the topic, and to engage in increasingly sophisticated discussions with their classmates. The activities you plan need to provide pupils with clear aims and purposes for their talk, clear structures to guide their work and clear outcomes so that they know what they are expected to achieve. The following case study illustrates this.

> ## Case Study: Planning for progression in oral activities
> Figure 4.4, overleaf, shows part of a medium-term plan developed by a trainee teacher on the popular classic narrative poem *The Highwayman*, followed by two extracts of talk from different activities in the unit of work. The plan was designed to be carried out over two weeks with a Year 5 class. Notice how the key learning objectives are in terms of pupils' understanding and knowing, and how they are
>
> →

linked with the outcomes, which are in terms of what pupils will be able do (at different levels, of course) at the end of each set of activities. Notice also how there is a strong focus on oral work, and a mix of whole-class and group activities across the plan.

Key learning objectives	Main activities	Resources	Assessment/ outcomes
Understand the structure and key features of narrative poems, and ways of performing them	Introduce *Highwayman* poem with pictures and artefacts – focus on setting, events, characters (mainly whole class, some group work) Develop performance of whole poem, in groups	Story sacks, artefacts from poem, pictures on IWB Audio or video recorder to record performance	All pupils take part in performance of poem
Understand the differences between literal and figurative language	Pupils in groups explore different characters in poem (using drama techniques) Pupils in groups explore literal and figurative language used to describe characters, write prose description of their own character Pupils consider main events in the narrative from range of viewpoints, and write narratives from different viewpoints	Large cut-outs of different characters from poem, thesauruses, dictionaries, simple props for role-play work	All pupils produce a piece of narrative writing based on the poem

Figure 4.4 Medium-term planning for 'The Highwayman'

Here are two examples of talk, one from the start of the plan and one from halfway through. Read them and then reflect on them using the questions in Activity 4.3 (see below). The first example of talk comes from the first lesson the trainee taught. She was introducing the poem to her class, and began by discussing the history of roads and stagecoaches, and the ways that highwaymen held up coaches. After this, she showed her pupils pictures of the characters and setting of

→

the poem (the pictures by Charles Keeping are excellent) and then read the first section to them. She wanted to make sure that her pupils had remembered the main facts of the poem, so she led a whole-class discussion.

Teacher:	Who do you think is the main character in the poem?
Child 1:	The highwayman.
Teacher:	That's right...who are the other important characters?
Child 2:	Bess, the black-eyed daughter.
Teacher:	That's right, and who else?
Child 3:	Tim, the ostler.
Teacher:	Who can tell me what an ostler is?
Child 1:	Someone who looks after the inn.
Teacher:	Not quite...he works in the stables, so he looks after the...
Child 4:	Horses.
Teacher:	That's right. Who can find a simile to describe Tim the ostler?
Child 3:	Hair like mouldy hay.
Teacher:	That's right.

The second example of talk came in the middle of the second week of work. The class had rounded off the first week by carrying out a performance of the whole poem, which had been videoed, and which they enjoyed very much. Following this, the pupils had been divided into mixed ability groups, and each group was given a different character to study. They did **hot seating** activities in their groups to explore the decisions made by their characters in the poem. Following this, the teacher re-organised the groups, so that each group included pupils who had studied different characters (this is called **jigsawing**). Each jigsaw group was given a different section of the poem to discuss from the viewpoints of the different characters, in such a way that the whole poem was covered. Then the class came together to review their findings about the different characters. This was to be followed in the next lesson by a writing task – each pupil was to plan a piece of writing where they wrote a narrative from the point of view of one of the characters in the poem; Bess, the landlord's beautiful daughter, Tim the ostler, King George's men or the highwayman himself. Here is part of one jigsaw group's discussion – they were talking about the end of the poem, after King George's men had killed the highwayman.

Child 1:	I don't think the highwayman should have come back for her, he should have known he would get killed.
Child 2:	But how was he to know that King George's men would come to the inn and set a trap for him?
Child 1:	It was really sad when he died...they shouldn't have killed him.
Child 3:	I think he deserved to die, highwaymen killed a lot of people...It shows you about Dick Turpin in York Museum and how he killed people on the roads.

$\rightarrow$

Child 1:	But he really loved Bess, and he made a promise to her.
Child 3:	He should have realised that they would be out to get him
Child 2:	They shouldn't have killed Bess the black-eyed daughter as it wasn't her fault.
Child 4:	They should have got Tim with the tatty hair.

Activity 4.3

Planning for collaborative talk, understanding *The Highwayman*

When you have read the two discussions, think about the following questions.

1. Which quadrants in Cummins' framework do you think the discussions fit into?
2. What do you think are the teacher's objectives in the first discussion?
3. What roles do the pupils take in this discussion?
4. What do you think the teacher needed to do in order for the pupils to take part in the second discussion?
5. What role does the teacher take in this discussion?
6. What roles do each of the four participating pupils take in this discussion?
7. What are some of the differences between the kinds of language the pupils use in each extract?
8. Do you think the second discussion is successful? Why?

In the *Highwayman* activities, there were several different kinds of groupwork.

- *Whole-class*, with a teacher-led question and answer session.

- *Mixed ability groups*, where pupils were sharing ideas about something they all knew about.

- *Mixed ability (jigsaw) groups*, where pupils had to share knowledge about different parts of the poem.

At other points in the *Highwayman* plan, the children would be engaged in different kinds of group work in order to complete different tasks.

- *Talking partner (pairs)*, for recalling and reinforcing knowledge and sharing ideas quickly at different times.

- *Friendship groups*, for the oral performance.

- *Ability groups*, for the writing task, so that support could be provided to meet the different needs of the children.

Other ways of grouping your pupils could be as follows.

- *Pair to four*: children are given a task to do in pairs, and then join up with another pair to make a group of four to share their findings – this can be a good way to form mixed-sex groups by having the pairs same-sex, then joining pairs of boys with pairs of girls.

- *Listening triads*: three children work together. Child A and child B carry out a task, which could be following instructions, telling a story, etc. Child C's role is to be the observer. They have to make careful notes of what is said, then report back to the rest of the class in the plenary part of the lesson.

2.2 Including new arrivals in your lessons – buddies and mentors

One of the main decisions that a teacher needs to make when a new-to-English pupil arrives in their class is what ability group they should join. Many teachers feel intuitively that new arrivals will be best placed in a low-ability group, perhaps because they feel they will be supported by additional staff and the activities will not be too demanding. But new arrivals are not necessarily of low ability and they may be hampered in their learning – and also feel that their prior knowledge and experiences are not valued – if they are not given interesting things to do which provide some cognitive challenge. It is often better to place new arrivals in a middle-ability group, so that they can begin to tune in to the discussions taking place and pick up models of classroom language.

As they settle into school and their social English begins to develop, new arrivals need to hear academic English being used fluently and competently in the development of learning. It is often a tricky balance to provide new arrivals with cognitively demanding activities at the same time as supporting them in understanding and using the language that this might entail. One of the key implications of this is that new arrivals must never be assigned to a group permanently. Their progress needs to be monitored to make sure they are being challenged. They need to be moved to a different group if it helps. They must also have the opportunity to mix with other pupils and engage in activities with different levels of language challenge.

It is often helpful to team a new arrival with a buddy or peer mentor. This may be a child who speaks the same home language and is more fluent in English and can therefore communicate readily as well as translate, or it may be a 'monolingual' child who is confident and curious and willing to assume responsibility for someone else for a while. The buddy's role could be shared by different children. For example, a 'language buddy' may be someone who shares the same first language as the child and who can act as an interpreter. If there is no other child in the class who can do this, the language buddy could be from another class or even a sibling or other relative who does not attend the school, but who comes in from time to time. Then, there may be a 'school buddy' who helps with getting to know the routines of the school, where things are, when things happen and so on. There may be a 'learning buddy', or different ones for different lessons or areas of the curriculum. The kinds of things buddies can do include:

- help familiarise the new arrival with where things are such as toilets, cloakrooms, dining hall, assemblies;
- explain who's who in school and what they do, e.g. secretaries, dinner ladies, TAs;
- support the new arrival in making friends;
- introduce the new arrival to other members of the school.

2.3 Planning for using home languages in learning

Research Focus: Home languages in mainstream classrooms

Charmian Kenner and colleagues have researched the ways that bilingual pupils in Tower Hamlets use their different languages for learning, and their attitudes to using different languages in the classroom. They found that children want to be able to use their home languages for learning in school, and that working in both languages can enhance children's learning, in the following ways.

- Understanding a concept in one language can be used to help a similar idea in another language.

- Mathematical concepts, in particular, are enriched by thinking in more than one language.

- Bilingualism gives children a heightened understanding of how language works.

- Bilingual activities give children the chance to draw on the full range of their cultural knowledge.

(Kenner et al., 2008)

Research such as this is clearly linked to the sociocultural theories of learning introduced in Chapter 2 as well as the ideas about bilingualism introduced in Chapter 3. It shows the importance of thinking about the languages and cultural knowledge that bilingual and EAL learners bring as resources for their learning of English and of other subjects across the curriculum. There are many ideas in Chapter 5 about ways of doing this. You can also think of ways, through your planning and organisation, to provide spaces in your classroom for children to use their full knowledge of languages to support their learning. For example, children could be grouped for part of the time in same-language groups where they discuss and plan an activity. Then they would be expected to feed back to the rest of the class in English.

Learning Outcomes Review

Together with the principles introduced after Chapter 3, the learning outcomes for this chapter give you some criteria to evaluate your planning to ensure that you have used every opportunity you can to promote learning for your bilingual and EAL learners in the activities you provide for them. To review how well you have understood the ideas in this chapter and used them to underpin your own planning, use the following checklist to evaluate your planning in any subject area of the primary curriculum. This will help you to see how far you have been able to find ways to promote learning for your bilingual and EAL learners, and also to identify points in your plans where you could improve provision. If you do this for one element of your planning, you could work with colleagues to evaluate all the planning for your class, year group or key stage.

> **Planning checklist – in your planning, have you:**
> - clearly identified the language demands of the activities (not just the key vocabulary, but the kinds of structures and texts that pupils will be using)?
> - included content that will be meaningful, relevant and interesting to your pupils?
> - made links with your pupils' prior knowledge in terms of both language and content?
> - made sure that the sequence of your activities supports your pupils' progress from context-embedded, cognitively undemanding learning to more cognitively demanding and less context-embedded learning?
> - provided plenty of opportunities for speaking and listening in ALL your activities, not just the introductory ones?
> - identified ways in which your bilingual and EAL learners could use their home languages for their learning?
> - planned different kinds of group work to provide opportunities for your pupils to engage actively with the concepts and content they are learning?

Further Reading

Gibbons, P. (1998) Classroom talk and the learning of new registers in a second language, *Language and Education*, 12:2, pp. 99–118.
This article, along with other materials written by Pauline Gibbons, gives very clear examples of the ways that concept learning and language learning go side by side, and how teachers can scaffold children's learning through oral activities across the curriculum.

Gravelle, M. (ed.) (2000) *Planning for bilingual learners: an inclusive curriculum*, Stoke-on-Trent: Trentham Books.
This helpful book includes a comprehensive and clear introduction which outlines principles for planning, and chapters written by different experienced teachers which give examples of planning for new arrivals and for learning across the curriculum.

References

Conteh, J. (ed.) (2006) *Promoting learning for bilingual pupils 3–11: opening doors to success*. London: Paul Chapman.

Gravelle, M. (1996) *Supporting bilingual learners in schools*. Stoke-on-Trent: Trentham Books.

Hall D., Griffiths D., Haslam L., and Wilkin Y. (2001) *Assessing the needs of bilingual pupils: living in two languages*, 2nd edn. London: Fulton Books.

Kenner, C., Gregory, E., Ruby, M. and Al-Azami, S. (2008) Bilingual learning for second and third generation children. *Language, Culture and Curriculum* 21:2, pp. 120–37.

NALDIC (2011) *Making the maths curriculum more accessible: strategies for children learning EAL* www.naldic.org.uk/ITTSEAL2/teaching/MathematicsPrimary.cfm (accessed 20 February 2012).

Wells, G. and Chang-Wells, G.L. (1992) *Constructing knowledge together: classrooms as centers of inquiry and literacy.* Portsmouth, NH: Heinemann.

5. Strategies and resources for learning across the curriculum

> ## Learning Outcomes
>
> This chapter will help you to achieve the following learning outcomes:
>
> - develop understanding of ways of linking language learning and content learning for bilingual and EAL learners in primary classrooms;
> - gain some practical ideas for using bilingual and EAL learners' linguistic and cultural 'funds of knowledge' to promote their learning;
> - develop awareness of the diverse ways in which stories can be used to promote learning across the curriculum in primary classrooms.

Introduction

This chapter provides practical examples of strategies and resources to promote bilingual and EAL children's learning across the curriculum in primary classrooms. They are all based on the theories about language, bilingualism and learning discussed in Chapters 2 and 3, and the principles listed at the end of Part 1 of the book. Cummins' ideas related to BICS and CALP were introduced in Chapter 3 and they underpin the examples in the first section of this chapter, which give you some ideas about linking language learning and concept/content learning in different subjects across the curriculum. There are also some suggestions for working with bilingual colleagues. 'Funds of knowledge' was introduced as a concept in Chapter 3 to explain the importance of home and family learning and experiences for children's success in school. The practical examples in section 2 of this chapter show you ways that funds of knowledge can be used in the classroom to help promote learning. This is followed by a discussion about the importance of story for children's learning across the curriculum in primary schools, and some practical examples of the ways that a familiar story can be used to promote learning in literacy.

All of these approaches are particularly valuable for bilingual and EAL learners, as they ensure that their learning is always grounded in meaningful contexts and experiences. At the same time, they are equally valuable for all children in primary schools. Throughout the chapter, there are discussion points and activities to help you think about the ideas you are reading about, and there are some suggestions for further reading at the end of the chapter.

These are the main sections and subsections of the chapter:

1. Linking language learning and content learning

- Focusing on language demands

- Working with bilingual colleagues

2. Using 'funds of knowledge'
- Bringing home languages and cultures into school

- Dual-language books

3. Using stories as a resource for learning
- Stories for language learning

- Using familiar stories creatively

1. Linking language learning and content learning

1.1 Focusing on language demands

The key principles for planning emphasise the importance of speaking and listening and of hands-on activities to provide primary children with rich opportunities for learning that can meet individual needs in a range of ways. Equally important is the need to think carefully about the language demands of the activities you are planning for your pupils. This means asking two key questions.

1. What language is involved in the particular concept and/or content that is the objective of the learning?

2. How can children be supported through the activity in developing their understanding and capacity to use the language independently?

We can think of language demands, essentially, in two ways. First, children need the key vocabulary – the words – that underpin the concepts they are learning. Second, they need to understand the words in context – in other words, in whole texts.

Words, words, words
Many words in English have different levels of meaning or different meanings in different contexts. This can be confusing for all children (and many adults), not just EAL learners. Think of the meaning of the word '*relief*' in a geography lesson, or on a bottle of cough medicine. Think of the word '*materials*' in a science lesson or in a dress shop. Think of words that we use every day in particular phrases that can seem contradictory – *running fast* is about moving quickly, but *sticking fast* is about staying still. Many words have everyday meanings that children will be familiar with, but then very particular meanings in school subjects.

....

Research Focus: The meaning of 'half'

One of the early KS1 mathematics SATs questions (for seven-year olds), set in 1997, was about children having soup for lunch. On the test paper, there was a simple picture of four children sitting round a dining table with bowls of soup in front of them. The question read something like, 'Half the children had chicken soup and half the children had tomato soup. Draw a circle round half the children.' The examiners were surprised to find that almost 70% of the children who took the test got this problem wrong, as mathematically it was not difficult. When the scripts were analysed, it was found that many children had drawn a circle round half of each child in the picture, rather than two out of the four children.

(Example from an examiners' moderation meeting)

....

All children, and particularly bilingual and EAL learners, develop **semantic** strength and capacity by having the opportunity, in a language-rich environment, to play with words, to encounter words in a range of contexts and texts and to make their own connections in word meanings. Here are some simple activities and ideas that can make your classroom a language-rich environment and encourage your children to be enthusiastic, curious and analytic about words and their meanings.

- *Displays:* find as many ways as possible to have relevant vocabulary on display round your classroom – word mats, word walls, labels, word banks and so on. Change them regularly to maintain children's interest. From time to time, mix up the labels and have children sort them out. Use bilingual lists and labels whenever you can. Ask your bilingual children to provide equivalent words and encourage your class to compare the different words for particular things and ideas.

- *Washing lines:* this is a good activity to reinforce children's understandings of words and develop awareness of shades of meaning. Prepare sets of words that show different degrees of meaning, e.g. size (*minuscule, tiny, small, middling, big, huge, gigantic*); volume (*whisper, mutter, mumble, grunt, shout, scream, screech*). Other categories could be heat; probability; speed; and so on – relate your words to concepts and content that the children are learning across the curriculum. Children in groups put the words in order, discussing and justifying their choices. Then they stand in line, so the class can see the words, and explain their decisions. Finally, the words are pegged on a washing line strung across the classroom so that everyone can see them and use them in their speaking and writing.

- *Odd one out:* this activity is based on sets of three or four words, which all have something in common, but there is always a feature shared by two but not all three. Here are some examples.

- *Sea, river, canal:* they are all bodies of water, but 'sea' is the odd one out because it has three letters; 'canal' is the odd one out because it is man-made; and 'river' is the odd one out because it has a 'v' in it.

- *Knight, sword, stone:* they are all from traditional stories, but 'knight' is the odd one out because it does not begin with 's', 'stone' is the odd one out because it ends with a vowel and 'sword' is the odd one out because it is made of metal.

- *Bird, fly, feather:* they are all to do with birds, but 'fly' is the odd one out because it is a verb and the others are nouns; 'feather' is the odd one out because it has four phonemes and the others have three; 'bird' is the odd one out because it ends in a consonant sound.

As you can see, there can be a range of answers, to do with phonics, spelling, meaning or grammar. The important point is that children have to explain and justify their own answers. Groups of children can be given sets of words to discuss and come up with answers, then the words can be given to another group. Once they get the hang of it, children can be asked to come up with their own sets of words to challenge their classmates. One of the benefits of this game is that it encourages children to think of meanings above individual word level, and so they develop understanding of texts.

Words, sentences and texts

As we saw in Chapter 2, words cannot be fully understood in isolation. The key vocabulary is not enough to help children develop the deeper understandings that are needed to promote the academic language required for real, powerful learning and achievement. Children need rich experiences of words used in a wide range of authentic texts in order to develop as capable speakers, readers and writers. They need to analyse texts in order to understand how they work and how to make the right choices in their own writing. The '5Ws' questions introduced in Chapter 2, linked to the functional approach, are helpful in analysing the language demands of the concepts and content that children are learning across the curriculum.

A key principle here is to make your literacy teaching cross-curricular, especially when you are teaching about non-fiction text types. Use topics for children's writing from different areas of the curriculum in which the children already have practical experience and knowledge. This will help to make their writing meaningful, authentic and purposeful. For example, after studying electricity in science, children can write instructions to make a circuit in literacy. After finding out about the Vikings in history, they can write a newspaper report about a raid on a village.

Here are some ideas for activities, which, in a language-rich learning environment, help children to develop academic language and independence as readers and writers.

- *Reference texts:* don't depend on computer dictionaries and spell-checkers – they often contain errors and children need to develop strategies for using reference texts including dictionaries, thesauruses and so on. Make sure you have a range available in your classroom, including picture dictionaries, bilingual dictionaries and subject dictionaries. Model their use with the children, and encourage them to use them independently in checking their spellings and finding the best words to express what they want to say or write.

- *Text frames (graphic organisers):* these are usually employed as supports to help children structure their written texts. They can also be a useful resource for developing reading skills and understanding of academic language. They are a visual way of helping children understand the ways that ideas are linked in different texts, and how to report, explain, justify, discuss and argue about the concepts they are learning. Alice Washbourne (2011: 124-5) provides some simple examples of graphic organisers to illustrate cause and effect, processes, cycles and so on, which children could complete after a science task with the information they have learnt, or after reading a non-fiction text in a particular **genre**.

- *Text reconstruction:* sometimes called **DARTs** (directed activities related to texts), are activities where children are expected to put back together a text that has been disrupted in some way. They are all about getting children to think beyond word level about what they are reading. They provide excellent opportunities for discussion, as an introduction to writing. A text can be cut into sections, and children have to work in a group to agree on how it goes together again. Children can be given the first part of a sentence, and then asked to choose the correct ending from a selection on the interactive whiteboard (IWB). Again, the emphasis needs to be on their explaining and justifying their choices.

Activity 5.1

Content and language

Choose a short non-fiction text from a topic you are planning to teach or a book or other resource you are using in your teaching. Using the 5Ws, analyse the type of text it is and consider what language demands it would place on EAL learners. Prepare a graphic organiser that would help children analyse and understand the text.

If possible, try your ideas out with a group of children; review and adapt for use in a future lesson.

1.2 Working with bilingual colleagues

There are many ways of using home languages and cultural experiences to help open out children's conceptual understanding in subjects across the curriculum.

In a school with a positive, welcoming ethos, knowledge of languages is seen as something to be celebrated and – more importantly perhaps – to be shared as a resource to use in strategies that promote children's learning. Bilingual colleagues have an important role to play in this. Bilingual teachers are still very much in the minority in mainstream schools in England. Their importance is not just in supporting the learning of their pupils, but also in raising all children's awareness of the importance of bilingualism in our society and as a role model of the positive benefits of bilingualism.

It is more common to have bilingual teaching assistants or support assistants who work alongside the teacher and support individual or small groups of children. Their presence can benefit the whole class. Virani-Roper, in Gravelle (2000: 73–4) has some lovely examples of the ways that bilingual assistants can link content teaching and language teaching in maths and also provide a bridge for parents. Here are some suggestions of ways of working with bilingual colleagues.

- Tell a story in two languages.

- Jointly assess children in different areas of the curriculum in order to evaluate their conceptual understanding as well as their language.

- Jointly plan an activity where you identify the language demands and think of ways that the concepts could be introduced bilingually.

- Ask your bilingual assistant to prepare materials to be sent home, which explain some of the things you have done in school, and also how parents can support their children at home.

The following case study illustrates good collaboration between bilingual colleagues. A trainee used his own basic knowledge of French to help a child new to English to engage actively in a science task. With the support of the school's PMFL teacher, who was a French specialist, he was able to support the child in showing how much he understood about the concepts being developed in the lesson.

Case Study: Working with bilingual colleagues

Ben undertook his first block placement on his PGCE course in a Year 3 class in a large school where most of the children were second- or third-generation Pakistani heritage. There was one 'new to English' child in the class, also of Pakistani heritage, but recently arrived from France where members of his extended family lived. Ben discovered that the child was fluent in French as well as Urdu. The class were doing a science topic where they were exploring the qualities of different materials, and Ben had prepared a recording sheet for the children to write down their findings about different objects in the classroom. With the help of the teacher responsible for PMFL, Ben wrote a French translation of the questions and statements above the English version on the sheet for the new pupil. The child was then able to carry out the investigation himself and write the names of the objects and some descriptive words in French on the sheet. In this way, Ben could appreciate his pupil's understanding of the science concepts in the activity, at the same time as providing a link for him to learning the words in English. Figure 5.1 shows the sheet which the child produced, with the teacher's writing above each question and the child's answers in the relevant spaces.

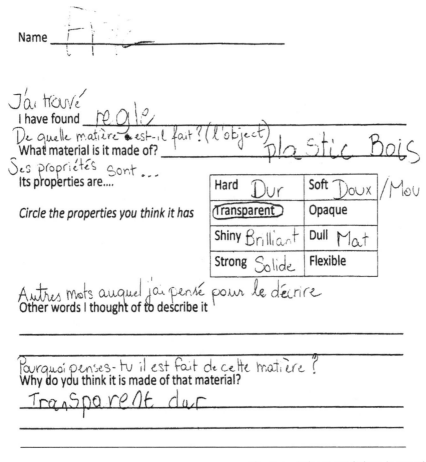

Name _Fi_____

Jái trouvé
I have found _regle_

De quelle matière *est-il* fait? (l'object)
What material is it made of? _____ plastic Bois

Ses propriétés sont ...
Its properties are....

Circle the properties you think it has

Hard Dur	Soft Doux /Mou
(Transparent)	Opaque
Shiny Brilliant	Dull Mat
Strong Solide	Flexible

Autres mots auquel j'ai pensé pour le décrire
Other words I thought of to describe it

_____

_____

Pourquoi penses-tu il est fait de cette matière?
Why do you think it is made of that material?

Transparent dur

_____

_____

Figure 5.1 Science worksheet in French and English

2. Using 'funds of knowledge'

2.1 Bringing home languages and cultures into school

The first point to emphasise in this section is that, while it is certainly very helpful if you can speak even a little of the home languages of the children you teach, it is not really a disadvantage if you can't. It is much more important that you have a positive attitude towards the language diversity of your pupils, and that you understand something of the ways that their knowledge of other languages influences their learning of English and how their cultural knowledge can be used as a positive learning resource. This said, it will promote a positive and welcoming classroom ethos if you can say a few words in some of the languages spoken by the children in your class – even to say 'hello' in his or her language will make a child's face light up and make them feel included in the class. The 'monolingual' children in your class also benefit from such a welcoming approach to other languages. Awareness of the language diversity of their communities is a very valuable way to break down barriers and promote social cohesion.

Language and cultural diversity can become a feature of your classroom through interactive displays, through the stories you choose to read to the children, and in many other ways. Time can be found in PHSE to allow the children to bring in stories from home, news and information about family and community events and about family in other parts of the world. The school and classroom can visibly reflect the diversity and global connections of the community. One school I worked in had clocks in the reception area and in the classrooms set to the times of the countries of origin of the children's families. If children go on visits to extended family in their country of origin, this can be turned into a positive aspect of their education by asking them to find out information to tell the class on their return and to bring back artefacts, if possible. Once back at school, they can be encouraged to bring in photos and to talk about where they went and what they did. Having a map of the country visited available can be very helpful, so that routes can be traced and places identified. A family member could be invited in to the class to support the child in talking about their visit, or questions could be written down and taken home for parents to answer. This can lead to fascinating discussions, such as the one described in Conteh (2003: 42-4) about an unusual medical treatment witnessed by a Year 3 child on a visit to Pakistan.

Simple routines, such as doing the register in different languages, also promote awareness of language diversity; the children can respond to their names with a greeting in any language they know. If a child brings a new language to the class, they teach their classmates the greetings. This can be reinforced with a poster showing '*How many ways can we say hello?*', which is regularly reviewed and updated. I once visited a Year 3 class where a boy, keen to find a new greeting to add to the poster, met me at the door and asked, 'Miss, can you speak any languages?' As well as greetings, other simple language features can be brought into the class as part of whole-class routines and in sharing times, possibly during PHSE. Children find counting in different languages fun and interesting. Start off by introducing a way of counting up to five in another language to your pupils and then find out what languages the children themselves can count in. This can be surprising, as they may have been taught to count in their home languages by their grandparents or other family members. This project can grow and become an ongoing subject of interest, involving parents, research on the internet and a working wall display.

Another excellent activity, which links to literacy, geography and RE, is finding out about the children's names and their origins. The following case study illustrates this.

Case Study: Name tree

Lisa, a trainee on her final placement in a Year 1 class in a multilingual school, decided to make a 'name tree' as part of her literacy work. She began by making a large cut-out tree shape (without leaves) for the classroom wall. Then she showed the children a photo of her own daughter and told them what her name meant and why she was given it. After this, she gave each child a letter (previously agreed

→

with the class teacher and translated into some of the home languages of the children) and a leaf cut out of green paper to take to their parents. The letter gave brief information about the project and asked the parents to help their child to write their name on one side of the leaf, in their own language as well as English, and a sentence about what the name meant and why they were given it on the other. The parents were enthusiastic about the project, and the leaves soon began returning to the classroom, along with positive comments from parents, who noticed the name tree sprouting leaves (Figure 5.2). Lisa organised her literacy lessons to allow each child to stand up, show their leaf, give a brief explanation of their name and then attach it to the name tree. The teacher, TA and other adults in the class added their own names. When all the names were on the tree, Lisa invited the parents to come and see the completed name tree. She also prepared a presentation with the children about the project for a whole-school activity.

Figure 5.2 A name tree on display in a classroom

Activity 5.2

Reflection

In a small group, reflect on one of the case studies you have just read, either about the name tree or about the bilingual science activity. The following questions can help you think about it.

1. What do you think made it effective as an opportunity for learning?
2. What literacy learning objectives do you think the children achieved in the activity?

3. What are the implications for planning activities such as these as part of your teaching (look back at the principles for planning in Chapter 4)?
4. Think of similar activities you could do in your class, using your pupils' 'funds of knowledge' as a resource for their learning. If you can, plan and carry out a simple activity for your class to promote awareness of language diversity. Consult your class teacher about what might be a good starting-point.

Using family and community funds of knowledge in your teaching makes the learning engaging and meaningful for all your pupils, not just those who are bilingual or EAL learners. It can be done across the curriculum, not just in literacy. There are some excellent examples of topic work which allow children to explore their own communities' histories while achieving learning objectives for geography, history, RE, science, ICT, literacy and other subjects on the *Multilingual learning* section of the Goldsmith's Department of Educational Studies website (Goldsmith's, University of London, 2011). The *Rag trade* project is a particularly powerful example, and full details are on the site. It was carried out with Year 5 and 6 children in Tower Hamlets in east London, and linked both with the community's history and the current situation in Bangladesh, where most of the children's families came from.

The work began with finding out about the tailoring industry in the East End of London, which was being increasingly outsourced to Bangladesh, exploiting cheap child labour. Factories in London, which in the past had employed many of the children's grandparents, were closing down. In one activity, the children in London thought of questions to ask the child workers in Bangladesh. They decided to translate the questions into Bengali so the children could understand them. This is what they came up with.

Questions to send to children in Bangladesh

- Do they make clothes for themselves? *(Ora ki nijeder jonno kapor banai?)*
- Do they get enough money? *(Ora ki poriman poisha pai?)*
- If they don't get their work done do they get beaten? *(Ora jokhon kaj shesh korte pare na oderke ki mare?)*
- How do the children know how to make the clothes? *(Bachara ki bhabe kapor shilai korte jane?)*
- Why are the children doing the work when there are so many adults to do it? *(Boro manush thakte bachara keno kaz kore hoi?)*
- Where do the children live? *(Ei bachara kothai thake?)*
- How do the children feel about working? *(Bachader kemon lage kaz korte?)*
- What happens to the people when they get hurt while they are working? *(Kaz korar shomai betha pele manushra ki kore?)*
- How many minutes break do they get? *(Ora koto shomoi'er jonno biroti pai?)*

- Is this happening now? *(Egolo ki ekhon hoche?)*
- How can we help them? *(Amra oderke ki bhabe shahajjo korte pari?)*

These questions represent a powerful, authentic written text. They were sent to Bangladesh and the responses built into further topic activities. They demonstrate not just the children's understanding of the topic they were studying, but their strong emotional engagement and empathy with the people whose lives they were studying.

Another excellent website with many ideas for using funds of knowledge to develop learning across the curriculum is *Every picture tells a story* (University of Sheffield, 2007). In this project, families who had migrated to Sheffield shared their stories about objects in their homes, which had significance for their community and family histories. Ravina Khan, one of the contributors, was born in Yorkshire almost 50 years before the time of the project. She talks about shawls made from cotton grown by her father and given to her when she visited Pakistan for the first time at the age of 11. Discussing objects like these in the classroom could be the starting-point for topic-based work incorporating many areas of the primary curriculum. Such work offers rich opportunities for children from all cultural and language backgrounds to be experts in particular aspects of knowledge and learning. The website has many fascinating stories, and also a detailed, downloadable teachers' resource pack, which has a lot of ideas and suggestions for activities.

Activity 5.3
Diversity across the curriculum
Choose a topic from the history, geography, RE or science curriculum, and think of ways in which you could develop activities which key into children's funds of knowledge, starting either with a significant object, picture or a local issue. Look back at the principles for planning in Chapter 4 and devise two or three activities, which could be the starting-point for teaching the topic.

You could do this activity with a small group of classmates, and each take a particular curriculum area.

2.2 Dual-language books

Dual-language books are a powerful resource for learning in many ways. The University of East London (UEL) website (2004) is the best source of information and ideas, along with Raymonde Sneddon's book (2009, see further reading at the end of the chapter). Dual-language books are usually stories published in two languages, though there are a few information texts. Both languages can be shown on one page or the two languages can face each other on alternate pages. Books published in the UK generally have English as one of the languages and many publishers produce series of dual-language books where the same story is written in different languages, all along with English. Sets of these can be very useful in promoting language diversity. Children who are not speakers or readers of the languages concerned but who can read English can read and compare the texts of the story in the different languages.

The importance of helping children to develop a positive identity as learners was raised in Chapter 2, and dual-language books can be a very effective means to do this. The story of Mushtaq (Chapter 3) illustrates this clearly. Dual-language books made by the children themselves were a powerful way for him to use his knowledge of literacy in Bengali as a means to becoming a reader of English. Cummins' and Early's book *Identity texts* (2011) discusses the importance of dual-language books, reporting projects done round the world where they have proved to be 'an effective and inspirational way of engaging learners in multilingual schools'.

Research Focus: Dual-language texts

For children who can read their home language, dual-language texts can provide a means of learning English, as well as developing metalinguistic awareness, an important capacity for understanding and analysing academic language. Dual-language books can be useful for children who can speak but not read their home language. Discussing the pictures can help them follow the story and develop their understanding of the structure, character, setting and so on. An article on the UEL website, written by a teacher, Angelika Baxter, discusses her research into using dual-language books with children new to English and provides many practical ideas for ways of using dual-language books to promote literacy as well as raising children's self-esteem and identity as learners: www.uel.ac.uk/duallanguagebooks/newtoenglish.htm (accessed 20 February 2012).

Activity 5.4
Dual-language texts

Find out what you can about dual-language texts – Mantra lingua is one of the main publishers and they have an extensive website. If you are able to, get hold of some dual-language texts representing the languages of the children you are teaching and share them with a small group of children.

3. Using stories as a resource for learning

3.1 Stories for language learning

Stories are a powerful medium for language learning. Storytelling is often a familiar activity in the home at the earliest stages of learning. The stories that children hear are valuable dimensions of their 'funds of knowledge', often reflecting the cultural and historical experiences of their families and communities. The storytelling has equal value, whether done in English or the home language. Important insights about language, such as how meaning in all languages is conveyed via combinations of sounds, words, sentences and texts, and about story structures and themes are developed naturally and in enjoyable ways.

In many homes, the tradition of oral storytelling is still strong; young children take part in listening to stories – often from the family's heritage in their country of origin – told by grandparents or other family members. Whether oral or focused on a book, the experience gives children many starting-points for literacy. The stories provide experience of repetition, rhythm and rhyme, which are transferable from one language to another and are valuable ways for children to begin to access language patterns and meanings. This is important, not least because story has such a big place in school literacy where, from Year 1, pupils learn to analyse story settings, events, character, structure and language.

There are several websites from different projects that give you ideas and starting-points for using stories as a means of learning relevant to your own class and the community of your school. One website, *Translation nation* (Eastside Educational Trust, 2011), reports on activities where children tell stories in their home languages, building in ways of supporting their listeners if they do not speak the language. Here are some simple ideas from the website, which could be done in any classroom.

• Introduce the language first, explaining which countries around the world it is spoken in.

• Use pictures, artefacts, actions or sound effects as you tell/read the story to give some helpful clues as to what the story is about.

• After you have told the story in its original language, ask your listeners if they have any idea of its themes or characters from the clues you have given. Then fill in the gaps with a short summary in English.

The website contains many more ideas around using stories bilingually, which help promote self-confidence in bilingual and EAL learners as well as building foundations for their literacy learning and development. For 'monolingual' children, the experience of listening to a story told in another language is a valuable one in developing their language and cultural awareness. To provide them with a bit of support, you could give them a few points to listen out for before the story begins – it can be surprising how much they do understand.

3.2 Using familiar stories creatively

Children respond to stories on a variety of levels, intellectually, emotionally and imaginatively, and many come to the classroom with a variety of traditional stories – in some cases from a range of cultures and languages – in their heads. The use of familiar stories can be highly motivating in validating pupils' existing linguistic and cultural knowledge, even though the story may be encountered in a different language. Prior familiarity with plot helps pupils work out the meanings of unfamiliar words. Well-known, traditional stories can be used in interesting and imaginative ways with children to achieve high levels of literacy learning, even with children in Years 5 and 6.

Case Study: Little Red Riding Hood in different countries

As part of their literacy teaching on their first school placement, two trainees, who were in a Year 5 class where about 70% of the pupils were bilingual, were asked to teach the Primary Literacy Framework unit of work *Stories from other cultures*. They began by finding several different versions of the *Little Red Riding Hood* story, and discussed these with the children, thinking about the differences in settings, characters and plots. They identified the key features of the story, then moved on to think about the ways it could be changed to fit into different countries and language and cultural contexts. Then the children developed Little Red Riding Hood fact sheets for different countries, such as that shown in Figure 5.3.

Figure 5.3 Children's fact sheet about France

→

The children were then arranged in groups and each group given a country and its fact sheet. The task was for the group to write the story of Little Red Riding Hood for their country. They were allowed to use words from any languages they knew in their writing and provided with this writing frame to help them organise their ideas, as in Figure 5.4.

My Tale from Another Culture Story Choices

The country where
my tale will be set is _____

The place where the
characters live is _____

My character will
be wearing red_____

So her name will
be Little Red_____

In their language,
Grandma is called_____

The food she is taking
to her Grandma is_____

On her way to Grandma's
she goes through a _____

On her way she meets a friendly
(but secretly deadly) _____

Her Grandma lives in a _____

Little Red... is saved by a_____

Figure 5.4 Story frame for Little Red Riding Hood

Many children used words from their home languages, thinking carefully how to spell them in the English alphabet. They were learning French in MFL, and some of them used vocabulary they had learnt in these lessons in their stories. Figure 5.5 is one of the pieces of writing the children produced.

→

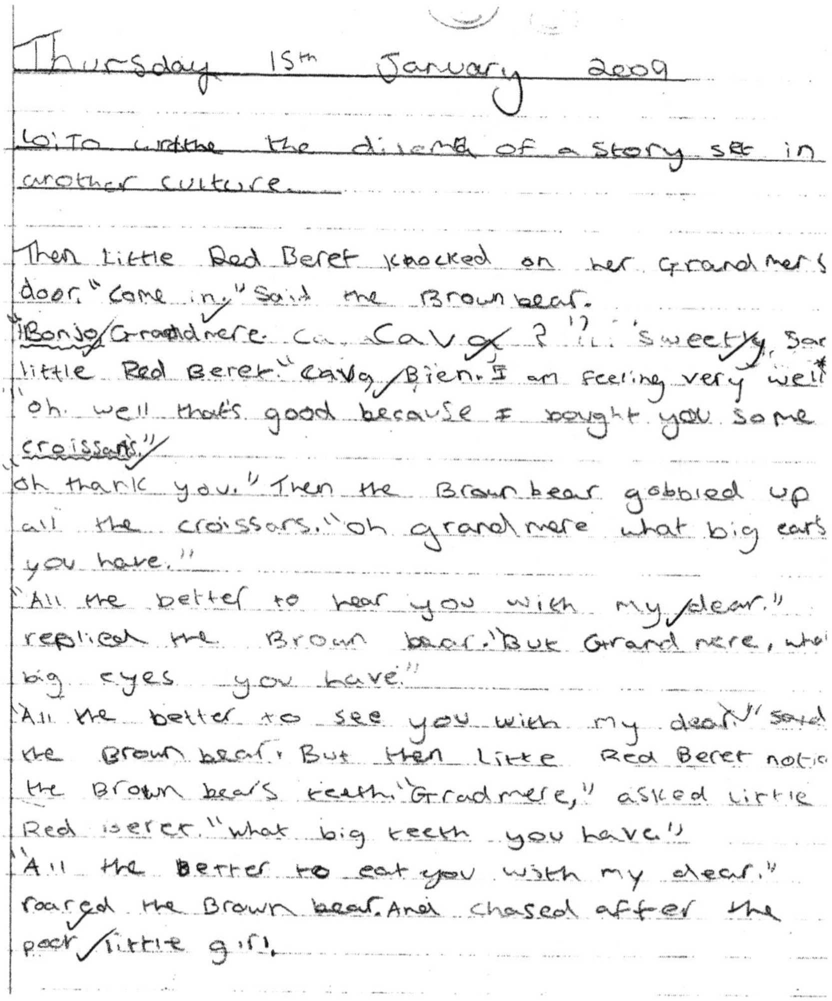

Thursday 15th January 2009

Lo: To write the diseng of a story set in another culture.

Then Little Red Beret knocked on her Grandmer's door. "Come in," Said the Brown bear. "Bonjo Grandmere. ca Cav gx?" "." "sweetly Sar little Red Beret." cavg, Bien. I am feeling very well "oh well that's good because I bought you some croissant."

"oh thank you." Then the Brown bear gobbied up all the croissors. "oh grand mere what big ears you have."

"All the better to hear you with my dear." replied the Brown bear. "But Grand mere, who big eyes you have."

"All the better to see you with my dear" said the Brown bear. But then Little Red Beret notic the Brown bea's teeth. "Gradmere," asked Little Red iseret. "what big teeth you have."

"All the Better to eat you with my dear," roared the Brown bear. And chased affer the poor little girl.

Figure 5.5 Child's 'bilingual' version of Little Red Riding Hood

Activity 5.5

Writing with traditional stories

Choose a familiar traditional story and think about how you could use it to develop some activities, which would help to improve bilingual and EAL learners' writing, using their knowledge of other languages.

If you can, try out your activities with a small group of children, then review and adapt so that they can be used in your future planning.

Learning Outcomes Review

The three learning outcomes for this chapter are all to do with linking the theories you read about in Chapters 2 and 3 to your thinking about the kinds of strategies and resources that will promote learning for your EAL and bilingual learners. You may be able to take some of the specific ideas described in the chapter into your own planning, but it is more likely that you will use your professional judgement to adapt them to your own classroom setting and the children you are teaching.

Self-assessment questions

1. As well as the examples discussed in this chapter, what other kinds of 'funds of knowledge' do you think could be used in your teaching across the curriculum?

2. *(If you are not bilingual yourself)* What issues do you think you might face in working with bilingual colleagues to promote children's learning? Think of some examples of ways in which you could work with a bilingual colleague, using your different expertise positively.

3. *(If you are bilingual yourself)* What issues do you think you might face in using your bilingual expertise to promote children's learning? Think of some examples of ways in which you could work with the children and with your colleague using your bilingual skills to promote learning.

Further Reading

Conteh, J. (ed.) (2006) *Promoting learning for bilingual pupils 3-11: opening doors to success.* London: Paul Chapman.

This book contains chapters written by teachers about projects they planned and carried out to promote listening and speaking with their bilingual and EAL learners. The examples show how they build a bilingual approach into their ongoing planning and teaching, not as an add-on. In this way, they open out the learning and promote independence in their pupils.

Sneddon R. (2009) *Bilingual books – biliterate children: learning to read through dual language books.* Stoke-on-Trent: Trentham Books.

Developed from action research work by primary teachers, this book features case studies of bilingual children aged from 6 to 10, and the ways in which dual-language books support their learning. It illustrates how young children can work simultaneously in two languages to read unfamiliar texts, and to analyse the differences between their languages. It offers ideas for teaching children languages as well as developing their bilingualism.

References

Conteh, J. (2003) *Succeeding in diversity: culture, language and learning in primary classrooms.* Stoke-on-Trent: Trentham Books.

Cummins, J. and Early, M. (eds) (2011) *Identity texts: the collaborative creation of power in multilingual schools.* Stoke-on-Trent: Trentham Books.

Eastside Educational Trust (2011) *Translation nation: inspiring literature in translation in primary school* http://translation-nation.heroku.com (accessed 29 January 2012).

Goldsmith's, University of London (2011) *Multilingual learning: complementary-mainstream partnerships* http://www.gold.ac.uk/clcl/multilingual-learning/cmp (accessed 29 January 2012).

Gravelle, M. (2000) *Planning for bilingual learners: an inclusive curriculum.* Stoke-on-Trent: Trentham.

University of East London (UEL) (2004) Dual language books: using and researching dual language books for children http://www.uel.ac.uk/duallanguagebooks/index.htm (accessed 29 January 2012).

University of Sheffield and others (2007) *Every object tells a story: family learning through objects in the home and in museums.* www.everyobjecttellsastory.org.uk/index.html (accessed 29 January 2012).

Washbourne, A. (2011) *The EAL pocketbook.* Management Pocketbooks Ltd. www.teacherspocketbooks.co.uk (accessed 23 April 2012).

6. Assessing bilingual and EAL learners across the curriculum

Learning Outcomes

This chapter will help you to achieve the following learning outcomes:
- understand the differences between standardised assessments of attainment and assessment for learning;
- understand the issues related to assessing the attainment of bilingual and EAL learners;
- understand the importance of assessment for learning for bilingual and EAL learners;
- gain knowledge of some practical strategies for assessing the strengths and needs of EAL and bilingual learners.

Introduction

In Chapter 3, some of the issues connected with developing an inclusive approach to assessment were raised. While it may be useful in some ways to be able to assess all children according to the same standards, if they are always assessed in the same standardised ways, the diversity of their experiences, knowledge and skills will not be recognised and understood. We may never find out about the things that individual children can do, which may be crucial to their ongoing development and learning. In order to plan the best opportunities for learning for bilingual and EAL learners, it is important to assess both their **achievements** and their **attainment,** in ways that recognise and value the full range of their experience, knowledge and skills.

This chapter begins by offering some key principles for assessing bilingual and EAL learners, taken from the QCA (2000) document *A language in common*. Following this, it raises issues about the standardised ways of assessing attainment, in order to meet official requirements and national standards, in relation to EAL and bilingual learners. In the third section of this chapter, there are suggestions for practical strategies to assess the learning and achievements of bilingual and EAL learners, using the outcomes to support their future learning. The EAL descriptors for KS1 and KS2 developed by **NALDIC** are introduced. These take account of the distinctive ways in which their knowledge of other languages and cultures may influence their learning of English and different subjects across the primary curriculum. Finally, there are some suggestions for ways of consulting with the parents and families of bilingual and EAL learners about their children's achievements and attainment.

Throughout the chapter, there are discussion points and activities to help you think through the ideas you are reading about, and there are some suggestions for further reading at the end of the chapter.

These are the main sections and subsections of the chapter.

1. Principles for assessing EAL and bilingual learners

2. Standardised assessments of attainment

- Issues in national assessment procedures for bilingual and EAL learners

- Language need or learning need?

3. Assessment for learning

- Profiling and sampling

- Assessment for learning – EAL descriptors for KS1 and KS2

- Observing

- Consulting with parents

1. Principles for assessing EAL and bilingual learners

The national tests of the attainment of all primary-aged children, the Standardised Assessment Tasks (SATs), were first introduced in the mid-1990s. At the time, there was a great deal of discussion about how to assess children who did not have English as their first language, as well as other children who were considered to have particular 'barriers to learning'. It was recognised that, for children new to English, it could be difficult to assess their understanding of different concepts, say in mathematics or science, without placing demands on their knowledge of English. So sometimes, it could be difficult to find out what children actually knew, in different subjects across the curriculum.

It was also recognised that the content of the tests could never be culture-free, and so there could be difficulties with comprehension or with the fairness of the tests. Certain content or ideas might be strange to children from different cultural backgrounds, or could be interpreted in different ways. Given what we know about the importance of contextual support for children's learning and for bilingual and EAL learners in particular, this presents something of a paradox – in trying to provide contextual support, we may actually be making things harder for some pupils. Zaitun Varian-Roper illustrates this beautifully in her chapter about mathematics in Gravelle (2000). Joshua, a child from Uganda, was asked the following question as part of a mathematics test:

> I ate half an apple and half of it was left. What was left? (p. 70)

Joshua's written answer was, 'seeds', and later he asked the teacher, 'But what is an apple, Miss?' There are clear sensitivities in this aspect of testing, and care must be taken not to make assumptions, which could lead to unwitting stereotyping or even racism.

These issues are general to all assessment. They will never be fully resolved, and must always be taken into account in interpreting the results of the SATs and other kinds of assessment. A document produced in 2000 by the Quality and Curriculum Authority (QCA) *A language in common* provides an excellent general overview of the language issues underpinning assessment for EAL and bilingual learners. It also makes suggestions for ways of taking their levels of language development into account. It begins by stating some principles for all teachers to consider.

- Be clear about the purposes of the assessment, distinguishing summative, formative and diagnostic aims.
- Be sensitive to the pupil's first or main other language(s) and heritage culture.
- Take account of how long the pupil has been learning English.
- Assess in ways that are appropriate for the pupil's age.
- Focus on language, while being aware of the influence of behaviour, attitude and cultural expectations.
- Recognise that pupils may be at different levels of attainment in speaking, listening, reading and writing.

(QCA, 2000: 8)

The first principle is crucial – it is vital to remember that you need always to be clear about the reasons why you are assessing children and what you intend to do with the outcomes. The remaining principles stress in different ways the importance of understanding about children's knowledge of other languages, and also their community and cultural contexts. They recognise that, for many bilingual and EAL learners, their learning of their new language of English may not be progressing in the same ways as children whose first language is English. For example, primary-aged children learning English as an additional language may quickly become competent and confident speakers, but their reading and writing may take much longer to develop. For some, particularly older pupils, their reading and writing may be much better developed than their speaking. In assessing bilingual and EAL learners, no matter what the subject area, always bear in mind their language experience and prior knowledge.

The recent *Bew Review* of testing at KS2 (DfE 2011a: 10–11) points out the dangers of trying to assess children's mathematical ability with questions where their reading capacity may prevent them understanding the maths required. This is, of course, an issue for many children, not just some EAL or bilingual learners. As suggested in Chapter 5, it can be very revealing to assess bilingual children's knowledge of mathematics or science in their first language, with the support of bilingual colleagues or older pupils.

2. Standardised assessments of attainment

2.1 Issues in national assessment procedures for bilingual and EAL learners

The SATs for children at the end of KS1 and KS2 are designed to test their attainments in English and mathematics in very specific ways. The 'fair test' cartoon in Chapter 3 raises issues about having one such universal means of assessing the attainment of every child in primary school. Not only does it mean that some children (like the fish or the seal in the cartoon) simply cannot do whatever the test might demand, but – just like the fish and the seal – they may have skills and expertise which the test does not recognise. It is crucial not to assume that because a bilingual or EAL child cannot do the standardised task, they cannot understand or do not know the concepts being tested. Over the years since the SATs were introduced, a wide range of intervention and assessment procedures have been developed, aimed to support the assessment of bilingual and EAL learners. These are often attached to funding arrangements in the same way that special needs assessments can lead to statementing. As Kimberley Safford's (2003) paper clearly demonstrates, they can often be very difficult and time-consuming to manage. And the outcomes may not always be very helpful for the children or their teachers.

Activity 6.1
Language and testing
Get hold of some old SATs papers for KS1 and KS2 in any subject. You may find some in school, or download some from this free website: http://freesatspapers. blogspot.com/2009/11/ks1-year-2-mathematics-sats-papers-and.html

Think about the language demands of the tests. Here are some points to consider.

1. Does the layout of the papers help or impair comprehension?
2. Are the instructions clear? Note down any you think may be difficult to interpret and think about how you might re-word them.
3. Is the wording of the questions clear? Are there any possible ambiguities or confusions?
4. Is the content of the questions appropriate? Can you identify any cultural issues or possible ambiguities that may cause problems?
5. Are the illustrations clear? Do they support the understanding of the questions, or make them more difficult?

2.2 Language need or learning need?

Since the Education Act of 1981 (DES, 1981), there has been a categorical requirement that children who speak other languages besides English at home must not be categorised *per se* as having special needs (SEN):

A child is not to be taken as having a learning difficulty solely because the language (or form of language) in which he (sic) is, or will be, taught is different from a language (or form of language) which has at any time been spoken in his home.

Despite this, there is often confusion between EAL and SEN. In assessing children, *language needs* can become interpreted as *learning needs*. EAL in itself can become constructed as a learning difficulty, which it is not.

Cummins' ideas about BICS and CALP, discussed in Chapter 3, need to be considered very carefully when deciding on the best approaches to assessment for bilingual and EAL learners. Children who speak other languages besides English at home or who arrive in school from another country, new to English, are often at earlier stages of acquiring English than 'monolingual' children of the same age. So they are behind their peers in this area of their learning. They often very quickly develop confidence and skill in conversational language (BICS), but their capacity to understand and use academic language (CALP) takes much longer to grow. Of course, it is also true that young 'monolingual' children are at the early stages of developing CALP too. But, because their acquisition of English is usually more advanced, they can move ahead more quickly in a classroom where English is the only means of communication and of learning.

If these aspects of language development are not well understood, there is a risk that the bilingual or EAL learner is assessed as having learning needs or *special needs,* whereas in fact they may more accurately have *language needs*. There may also be cultural factors that are affecting their learning, which the school or the child's teachers are not aware of. The answer to providing for their needs and promoting progress in their learning may not be to set them to do cognitively simplified tasks and give directed teaching of simple English. It may instead be much more helpful to ensure that they have the opportunities and the support (including using their home languages) to engage in increasingly cognitively challenging activities in contextually supported ways, as is suggested in the discussion on planning in Chapter 4. It may be helpful not to rush to intervene in any way, but simply to spend a bit of time in observing the child and thinking about his or her behaviour, as the following case study, taken from Gregory (2008: 20–1), illustrates.

Case Study: Tony – EAL and/or SEN?

Tony, a Chinese-heritage child who lived with his parents and grandparents, was very bright and eager when he joined the Reception class of his local school at the age of 4 years 10 months. For a while, all went well. He was very alert and constantly asked, 'What's that?', pointing to things in the classroom. This amused the teacher and reminded her of a much younger child. He loved to draw, and spent a long time carefully and methodically copying the covers of books. After a while, Tony changed. His enthusiasm seemed to evaporate, and he would wander

→

round the classroom aimlessly. His constant 'What's that?' worried the teacher, who began to think he lacked ability or was not getting encouragement from his family. A researcher who was studying Tony's literacy development visited his home. She was surprised by the frosty reception she received from Tony's grandfather, who showed her an exercise book with pages filled with rows of immaculately written Chinese characters. This was the product of Tony's work at the Chinese Saturday class he regularly attended. The grandfather compared this with a drawing Tony had done on the back of a shop advertisement, where he had written his name in poorly formed English letters, some capital, some lower case, in the corner.

At his Saturday class, Tony was clearly a capable and assiduous pupil, who could sit for long periods, carefully copying characters until the strokes were perfect, which is very important in Chinese calligraphy. At his mainstream school, he seemed unable to pay attention for a few minutes, and the work he produced often looked careless and messy. In discussing the home visit with the researcher, Tony's teacher began to understand that he was a very intelligent and hardworking child who needed to have the space to learn in different ways from the other children in the class, who were mostly 'monolingual'. Placing him in a special needs group would not help him develop to his full ability.

Activity 6.2

Reflection – EAL or SEN?

Consider the issues raised in the case study above about the possible confusions about Tony's needs and how to support him. Think about children you have worked with, who may have been identified as having SEN, and children categorised as EAL. Use these questions to reflect on the possible confusions between EAL and SEN.

1. From what you read above, how would you have assessed Tony's capabilities when he began school?
2. What might have helped the teacher to understand Tony's behaviour when he began school?
3. Why do you think Tony's grandfather was unhappy when he met the researcher?
4. What does the case study tell you about the ways that bilingual children might learn literacy and how does this relate to the theories you read about in Chapter 3?
5. What does the case study tell you about the links between home and school?
6. If you were Tony's teacher, what would you do, now that you know something about his experiences of literacy learning in his home community?

3. Assessment for learning

3.1 Profiling and sampling

In essence, assessment for learning is the process of making informed, diagnostic judgements about the children you teach, in order to decide what to do next. To help them make progress in a particular area of their learning, you need to know what your pupils can and cannot do. Collecting the information you need to make these judgements takes thought and time. Profiling and sampling are important assessment for learning strategies. With bilingual and EAL learners, the first and most essential kind of profiling you need to do should take place as soon as – or even before – they enter school, whether as a new pupil in Nursery or Reception, or as a new arrival further up the school. Hall et al. (2001) suggest the information that schools need to know about children's languages and cultural backgrounds, and they provide a useful photocopiable form (pp. 76–7), which could be used for the purpose. Ideally, this kind of information should be collected as part of normal, everyday whole-school routines, and made available to teachers. If this is not the case in your school, you could collect it in your classroom. Here is a slightly adapted version of Hall's list.

1. Name child is called at home

2. Name to be called in school (if different)

3. Place of birth

4. Arrival date in UK

5. Family members who the child lives with

6. Length of previous schooling (in country of origin, and elsewhere, including UK)

7. Religion and festivals observed

8. Languages spoken at home to:
   a. Mother
   b. Father
   c. Siblings
   d. Grandparents

9. Languages used by family members to child

10. Languages other than English that child can read/write

11. Is the child right- or left-handed?

12. Does the child attend any school or class in the community:
    a. Supplementary/complementary school
    b. Religious school
    c. Any other?

13. What languages are used and taught here?

14. Contact name(s) and details for the organisation(s)

15. Is an interpreter needed for teacher to talk to the parents?

16. If so, who and how can they be contacted?

Another aspect of profiling is the sampling of children's progress through the work they produce. This can be done for any subject across the curriculum, in different ways. The aim is to collect evidence of children's achievements at different stages of their learning of a particular topic or concept. Their development in speaking, listening, writing or reading can also be evaluated in this way to help you decide what to do to help them to make progress. The idea of sampling was one of the key principles behind the *Assessing Pupil Progress* (APP) materials (DfE, 2011b). For example, to assess a child's progress in writing, samples of their written work are collected over a set period of time. Then they are assessed according to criteria that lead not just to assigning a level, but also to indicating what can be done next, to promote learning.

The case study below (taken from Edwards, 1995) shows the rapid progress that can be made by a bilingual learner, in a supportive classroom environment where he is allowed to use his literacy in his first language to support his development in English.

Case Study: Shahed's writing

Shahed was ten years old when he arrived in England from Iran. He had a high level of literacy in Farsi, the official language of Iran, but very little English. For the first few months of his time in England, he was given the opportunity to write in Farsi while the other children in the class were doing their normal literacy activities. The teacher was able to find out what he wrote about with the help of his father. Figure 6.1 is an example of one of his early Farsi texts.

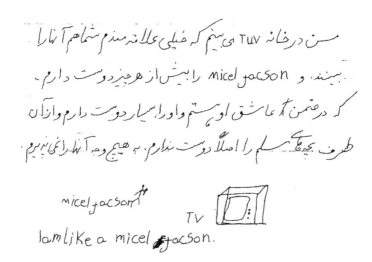

Figure 6.1 Shahed's Farsi writing

→

In common with many other biliterate children, Shahed is beginning to use his knowledge of different scripts to express his meanings in his writing.

After six months in the school, Shahed was still writing in Farsi, but his writing in English was developing fast. Figure 6.2 is taken from his writing journal.

I like my father and, He,is very Kind and my

mother very Kind, and she,is love me.mysisther

is very good girl andshe,is Kind .my mother is

working in the universityand my,

father going to the libery and He is Ridingthe

book and He Like book ,and He,is artist and

He taking to piupel.

END

Figure 6.2 Shahed's writing, six months later

Three months later, he was taking a full part in most lessons, and literacy was one of his favourites. In a lesson where the children had been looking at picture books in order to write a story for younger children, *Not now Bernard* by David McKee was a favourite. Shahed wrote a letter to Bernard's parents (see Figure 6.3).

dear Bernard's parents

it's better You are more Kind to Bernard and You sould

take him To park, fenfairs,...... .he can do any thing with

his salf, Canhe? if I was his parents, I take him To the

park or some were,any were he like, like cinema .

so dont Just say not now Bernard ! You can read a

story every night for him,or when he ask canh I stayed

at night to 8,9 o'clock 9 You can said to him,You can stayed

this night,but not after 9 o'clock ok 9 You canplay fot ball

in out said of your house with Bernard.

from:

Shahed

Figure 6.3 Shahed's writing, three months later

Activity 6.3

Assessment for learning and writing

Here are the Assessment Focuses for writing from the APP materials.

- AF1: Write imaginative, interesting and thoughtful texts.
- AF2: Produce texts that are appropriate to task, reader and purpose.
- AF3: Organise and present whole texts effectively, sequencing and structuring information, ideas and content.
- AF4: Construct paragraphs and use cohesion within and between paragraphs.
- AF5: Vary sentences for clarity, purpose and effect.
- AF6: Write sentences with technical accuracy of syntax and punctuation in phrases, clauses and sentences.
- AF7: Select appropriate and effective vocabulary.
- AF8: Use correct spelling.

Using the Assessment Focuses, analyse Shahed's two pieces of writing in English. Think about what he can do in each piece, and also what he seems to be trying to do. Think about these questions.

1. What progress do you think he shows from the first piece to the second?
2. What do you think are Shahed's strengths and weaknesses?
3. If you were his teacher, what would you do to help him make further progress in his writing?

3.2 Assessment for learning – EAL descriptors for KS1 and KS2

It must be remembered that the Assessment Focuses, and all the other elements of the *Assessing Pupil Progress* (APP) materials, which have been introduced nationally over the past few years, have been developed based on a model of monolingual development in listening, speaking, reading and writing. There are currently no nationally agreed assessment descriptors for bilingual and EAL children. NALDIC have developed two sets of descriptors, one for KS1 and one for KS2, which are easily downloadable from their website. They are not an alternative to the APP materials, but they provide useful indicators to help you recognise and understand the distinctive ways in which bilingual and EAL learners' listening, speaking, reading and writing develop. Used in addition to the APP materials, they will provide you with a full and informative overview of the progress of your bilingual and EAL learners, and where they need to go next.

3.3 Observing

In section 2.2 above, I mentioned the importance of observation for understanding the behaviour and learning of bilingual and EAL learners. It is particularly important to take as many factors into account as you can in your professional judgements, to ensure that you decide on the right provision to help children make progress. This is often the case when you are trying to assess the knowledge and understanding of bilingual and EAL learners. If a child is at an early stage of acquiring English and so has a limited capacity to produce spoken English, they may show their understanding of an instruction, an idea or a concept non-verbally. For example, watching carefully how a child places magnetic letters while trying to spell a word or how she physically writes on a whiteboard can reveal a lot about what they understand about letter sounds and symbols. In the same way, watching how they use their fingers or concrete resources when counting in maths can tell you a lot about their understanding of numbers and number bonds, which they may not be able to put into English words. More broadly, watching how a child interacts with other children, in the playground and in other settings besides the classroom at different points in time, can show you a lot about their overall language development, self-confidence and identity as a learner.

In many ways, observing is a key professional skill for all teachers, and you will quickly find that you are constantly making a mental note of things you observe or notice about a child. Get into the habit of writing down things that strike you as significant. In many Early Years classrooms, this is part of the routine and there are notebooks to hand so that staff can do this, and then collect up comments about individual children in a portfolio. This practice is not so common once children move into KS1 and KS2. But it is something you could introduce in your class. As well as this kind of spontaneous observing and recording, it is useful to arrange more focused observations from time to time in order to collect evidence about a particular child's progress, or evaluate a specific approach or strategy in your teaching.

Remember that in observing, as in any form of research, you must always act ethically and be sure to take account at all times of any ethical issues connected with the activity and the children involved. This is particularly important when you are a trainee, as you are working always under the guidance of others, who will take ultimate responsibility for your actions. Here are a few ethical points to consider when carrying out observations.

- Always seek 'informed consent' before beginning observation by making sure that children know you are observing them – teachers have responsibilities for protecting their pupils.
- Be aware of legal considerations and child protection issues.
- Make sure that confidentiality is maintained.
- Interpret and analyse – don't judge!
- Think about how you will use your findings – why are you carrying out the observation?
- What do you do if you observe something inappropriate or dangerous – to intervene or not to intervene?

The last point has clear links to safeguarding, and it is a good idea to check with your class teacher beforehand if there might be any sensitive issues related to a child you plan to observe. If anything did emerge during the course of the observation, for example, inappropriate behaviour or comments that come up in conversation, your role as a trainee teacher is to pass them on immediately to your class teacher and then withdraw from the situation. Any resulting action may need to be kept confidential and, as someone who is in the school for a limited period, you must not be involved.

Activity 6.4

Observing

During your next school placement, if possible, arrange to spend 20–30 minutes observing a bilingual or EAL learner in their classroom, in order to gain a sense of how they behave and participate in the classroom. Have a brief conversation with the child before you begin, so that they are aware of what you are doing. Here are a few 'dos and don'ts' to think about in setting up your observation.

1. Do remember to record contextual features – layout of classroom, organisation, lesson topic, resources used, etc.
2. Do set up a specific focus for your observation, e.g. a particular child, teacher's use of questions as a teaching strategy, etc.
3. Don't judge – only write down what you see and hear.
4. Don't observe for long periods of time – usually 10 minutes at a time is enough, then break for a minute or so, and then continue.
5. Do recognise your own biases and viewpoints – no observation is neutral.

3.3 Consulting with parents

Tony's story above reveals a great deal about the importance of finding out about a child's home and community experiences of learning and of literacy, a point that has been emphasised many times throughout this book. In terms of assessment, it can help you interpret what the child does in school in much more holistic ways and lead to much better informed decisions about what to provide for the child. As part of the assessment cycle, teachers also have the responsibility of reporting children's achievements to their parents, and providing an opportunity for them to discuss their child's progress. As a trainee, you may be involved in this, and you need to gain some experience in this area. An important issue in relation to bilingual and EAL learners is the need to make sure that the arrangements for reporting and consulting meet the parents' needs, which may differ according to their language and cultural backgrounds. In some families, it is not the parents who take the responsibility for communicating with the school about the child's education: it may be an uncle or aunt, or even an older sibling. There may be the need for an interpreter, which might be someone working in the school or someone from the community.

Learning Outcomes Review

The four learning outcomes for this chapter are about developing your understanding of the different purposes and types of assessment as a whole, as well as specific issues related to EAL and bilingual learners. The chapter also introduces you to some practical ways in which you can use assessment processes to support and promote learning for your bilingual and EAL learners. Thinking about school-based experiences you have had in general and with EAL and bilingual learners in particular, reflect on the learning outcomes using the questions below.

Self-assessment questions

1. What are the key differences between, assessment *for* learning and assessment *of* learning? What are the general issues related to each in assessing the achievements and attainment of EAL and bilingual learners?

2. Why do you think it so important that *learning needs* are not confused with *language needs* for bilingual and EAL learners?

3. Why are assessment for learning strategies, such as profiling and sampling, particularly important for bilingual and EAL learners? What specific issues have you faced (or might you face) in sampling the work of a child who is relatively new to English?

4. What factors may make consulting with parents of bilingual and EAL learners about their children's achievements and attainment different from consulting with the parents of 'monolingual' children, and how is it the same?

Further Reading

Briggs, M. (2011) Assessment, in: Hansen, A. (ed.) *Primary professional studies*, pp. 184–203. Exeter: Learning Matters.
This chapter provides a full overview of assessment and introduction to assessment for learning and assessment of learning in primary classrooms.

NALDIC (2009a) *Introduction to NALDIC formative assessment descriptors: an introduction to NALDIC's EAL assessment descriptors.* www.naldic.org.uk/Resources/NALDIC/Teaching% 20and%20Learning/NALDICEALFormativeAssessmentIntroductionfinal.pdf (accessed 3 March 2012).

NALDIC (2009b) *Assessment descriptors KS1: formative EAL assessment for KS1 EAL learners.* www.naldic.org.uk/Resources/NALDIC/Teaching%20and%20Learning/NALDICdescriptors KS1.pdf (accessed 3 March 2012).

NALDIC (2009c) *Assessment descriptors KS2: formative EAL assessment for KS1 EAL learners.* www.naldic.org.uk/Resources/NALDIC/Teaching%20and%20Learning/NALDICdescriptors KS2final.pdf (accessed 3 March 2012).

These three documents, which can all be easily downloaded from the NALDIC website (www.naldic.org.uk) provide a means of assessing the progress of bilingual and EAL learners in speaking, listening and reading.

Safford K. (2003) *Teachers and pupils in the big picture: seeing real children in routinised assessment.* Watford: National Association for Language Development in the Curriculum (NALDIC). www.naldic.org.uk/eal-publications-resources/Shop/shop-products/op17 (accessed 11 February 2012).
This paper, written by a teacher a few years ago, is very illuminating. It shows the complex and complicated processes that teachers often need to go through in order to meet official assessment requirements for bilingual and EAL learners, and makes some useful suggestions for really understanding their needs.

References

Department of Education and Science (DES) (1981) *Education Act 1981.* London: HMSO.

Department for Education (DfE) (2011a) *Independent review of Key Stage 2 testing, assessment and accountability: Final Report* (The Bew Review). https://media.education.gov.uk/MediaFiles/C/C/0/{CC021195-3870-40B7-AC0B-66004C329F1F}Independent%20review%20of%20KS2%20testing,%20final%20report.pdf (accessed 24 February 2012).

Department for Education (DfE) (2011b) *Assessing pupils' progress (APP) overview.* http://webarchive.nationalarchives.gov.uk/20110202093118/http://nationalstrategies.standards.dcsf.gov.uk/primary/assessment/assessingpupilsprogressapp (accessed 16 February 2012).

Edwards, V. (1995) *Writing in multilingual classrooms.* Reading and Language Information Centre, University of Reading.

Gravelle, M. (2000) (ed.) *Planning for bilingual learners: an inclusive curriculum.* Stoke-on-Trent: Trentham Books.

Gregory, E. (2008) *Learning to read in a new language: making sense of words and worlds.* London: Sage.

Hall, D., Griffiths, D., Haslam, L. and Wilkin, Y. (2001) *Assessing the needs of bilingual pupils: living in two languages*, 2nd edn. London: David Fulton.

Quality and Curriculum Authority (QCA) (2000) *A language in common: assessing English as an additional language.* QCA Publications. http://media.education.gov.uk/assets/files/pdf/a/a%20language%20in%20common%20assessing%20eal.pdf (accessed 2 February 2012).

7. Conclusions: synthesising learning and moving on

As with any aspect of becoming a primary teacher, your initial training can only give you an introduction to the professional attributes, knowledge and skills you need to understand bilingual and EAL learners' needs and make provision for their successful learning in your classroom. In this final chapter, you are invited to reflect on what you have learnt so far, at the start of your career. Through considering the knowledge you have gained from reading this book, as well other experiences you may have had on your course of training, you will synthesise your understanding of EAL in the primary school. Following this, you are invited to think about moving on in the development of your professional expertise in this important and growing aspect of the primary teacher's role. At the end of the chapter, there are suggestions for further reading. Do not forget, also, about the further reading suggestions at the end of each chapter in the rest of the book.

The whole field of EAL teaching and learning is a growing one that has relevance for all teachers. In recent years, it has increasingly become recognised that there is a body of both theoretical and practical knowledge that teachers need in order to develop language-based and culturally informed pedagogies, which see language diversity as a resource in primary classrooms. And it is becoming increasingly clear that such pedagogies are good for all children. They not only promote success for bilingual and EAL learners, but they also contribute to more positive attitudes generally towards language diversity and thus to greater cultural awareness. This, in turn, has positive benefits for social cohesion and justice in the wider community. There are exciting possibilities for newly qualified teachers, who have the interest in and the commitment to the positive, inclusive values that promoting EAL in this way offers, to become specialist teachers and future leaders in the field.

Myths revisited

In Chapter 1, four myths about language teaching and learning were introduced. I suggested that they needed to be challenged, as they represent commonsense, but often unhelpful, notions that are not supported by research about language and learning in relation to bilingual and EAL learners. In order to help you synthesise your knowledge and understanding about EAL, this section provides a brief reflection on each of the myths, showing how what you have learnt in this book reveals their shortcomings and suggesting positive ways of moving forward.

1. Languages should be kept separate in the classroom, or learners will become confused (sometimes called 'language interference')

In the first part of the book, there are a lot of ideas that call the 'language interference' myth into question. In Chapter 2, links are made between language and identity, which have relevance for all children – a child whose accent or dialect is ignored or treated as a form of 'bad' English is just as likely to feel excluded from the classroom as a bilingual child who is made to feel that it is unacceptable to speak any other language than English. Language, identity and learning are intimately connected, as the theories introduced in Chapter 2 show. In Chapter 3, the examples of 'translanguaging' from Sameena, as well as Cummins' theoretical idea of the CUP, and the definition of bilingualism as 'living in two languages' all show in different ways how it is wrong to construct children's languages as separate phenomena that must be kept apart. Similarly, the principle about linking home and school learning is illustrated by many different examples in Chapter 5. Dual-language books, cross-curricular work with artefacts, a worksheet in science with additional French words that 'opened up' the science concepts for a newly arrived child – these are all examples of practical ways to link languages in order to promote children's conceptual learning and bilingual language development.

2. Children will 'pick English up' naturally in the classroom; they do need to be explicitly taught (sometimes called 'immersion')

The vignettes of different 'EAL learners' presented in Chapter 1 show in a range of ways how children do not 'pick up' English in the classroom and somehow become successful learners without any conscious understanding and planning on the part of the teacher. For social and cultural reasons, Umaru was struggling to do as well as he had the capacity to do, and if his teachers had found out more about his background, this might have helped them to think about how to help him in more informed ways. Yasmin was doing very well in speaking and listening, but the evidence from schools such as hers is that she might find the written demands of the Year 6 SATs difficult. The contrasts between Stefan's and Jan's progress clearly indicate that it was not simply a matter of 'picking up' English for them.

Many of the questions raised by these examples are answered in Chapter 3 with Cummins' model of BICS and CALP, which explains some of the complexities of the development of academic language, essential for academic success. Then, all the detail about planning for both language and conceptual progression provided in Chapter 4 offers practical ways to ensure that children are offered carefully structured activities to support both their language and conceptual development. Chapter 5 gives many suggestions for providing a language-rich classroom environment and linking language and content in your teaching. Finally, Chapter 6 provides advice on assessing conceptual learning for children whose English development is at an early stage, as well as a way of understanding bilingual children's development as distinctive from children who are not learning bilingually.

3. Language diversity is a 'problem', and it is better if children speak English all the time in classrooms

In Chapter 1, it is established that language and cultural diversity have long been a feature of everyday life in Britain, and the signs are that they will always remain so. The children of Yasmin, Stefan, Jan, Umaru, Hamida and Radia, should they choose to remain in Britain and take up citizenship here, will be citizens of an increasingly multilingual and multicultural society. In Chapter 2, it is argued that we all experience language diversity in our daily lives, even if we think of ourselves as monolingual in English. Following this, in Chapter 3, the idea of bilingualism or multilingualism as a spectrum is presented. Some of us may place ourselves towards the 'monolingual' end of the spectrum in our experiences and knowledge of language diversity, and others may be towards the more expert, multilingual end, with high levels of competence in listening, speaking, reading and writing in different languages. In Chapter 5, there are many practical ideas for making language diversity a positive feature and resource in your classroom, no matter what languages are spoken by the children you teach. Simple activities like doing the register in different languages can be fun, promoting a positive ethos in a very accessible way and opening doors to learning about different languages for your pupils.

4. It is impossible, or very difficult, to learn a new language beyond a young age (sometimes called 'the critical period')

The vignettes in Chapter 1 show bilingual learners of different ages becoming competent and confident speakers, readers and writers of English. The important point to consider is that they do this in different ways, and so need different kinds of teaching and support. The example of Stefan and Jan, both from the same language background and in school in England for the same length of time, illustrates very clearly that there is no universal way to becoming a competent user of English. The learner's age is only one factor that must be taken into account, as are the languages they already know in both spoken and written modes. Mushtaq's story in Chapter 3 is a positive one that encourages us to have confidence in our pupils as independent learners. He quickly became a competent reader and writer of English, once his skills and capacity in his first language of Bengali were known.

All these examples illustrate how the idea of the 'critical period' in the sense of there being an age beyond which it is always very difficult to learn a new language is a myth. The distinctiveness of children's 'EAL development' at different ages must be understood. The descriptors developed by NALDIC, discussed in Chapter 6, offer an excellent starting-point for assessing individual children's progress as bilingual language users. They are also helpful in developing your own understanding of the distinctiveness of bilingual and EAL learners' development and progress.

Moving forward – some suggestions for further reading and professional development

A major concern of this book has been to help you to understand the importance of theory in your professional understanding and development as a primary teacher. Of course, theory by itself is of no value in teaching, but neither are lists of practical suggestions with no theoretical rigour behind them, and no evidence of the principles from which they have been developed. If you depend on these in your teaching, you will quickly run out of ideas and be at the mercy of ready-made plans with no real understanding of how and why they have been constructed in the way they have.

This book gives you a theoretical explanation for all the practical advice it provides. This is intentional – the hope is that you will be able to go on to develop your own theory-informed and principled ways to plan, teach and assess the learning of the children you teach, especially those who are bilingual. As you move into your induction year as an NQT, you could suggest to your school mentor that you use some of the activities in this book to help develop your professional expertise.

The further reading suggested at the end of each chapter gives you some starting-points for your CPD. The list given below, taken from the references for each chapter, will help you to move further in your understanding of how to integrate theory and practice in your teaching. Books speak to readers in different ways – these are all titles which have inspired me in my teaching and to which I have returned many times. I hope some of them will speak to you and, as well as offering you useful guidance for your teaching, showing you the importance of further study. As time goes on, you may be offered the opportunity or feel the need to pursue higher qualifications, and the study of EAL has rich potential. Use the NALDIC website (www.naldic.org.uk) – and join the association – to keep up to date with developments in the field of EAL, including opportunities for further study and professional development.

Suggestions for further reading

Cummins, J. (2001) *Negotiating identities: education for empowerment in a diverse society*, 2nd edn. Ontario, CA: California Association for Bilingual Education.
This book gives a thorough explanation of Cummins' theories introduced in this book – CUP, linguistic interdependence, BICS and CALP – and others. It show how all his ideas have developed over the years. The educational implications are fully explained.

Cummins, J. and Early, M. (eds) (2011) *Identity texts: the collaborative creation of power in multilingual schools*. Stoke-on-Trent: Trentham Books.
This book is a collection of case studies and examples of 'identity texts', which are texts created by EAL learners in a wide range of educational settings round the world. They illustrate how such work can contribute to a pedagogy that plays to the strengths of children from diverse language and cultural backgrounds.

Datta, M. (2007) *Bilinguality and biliteracy: principles and practice*, 2nd edn. London: Continuum.
This book shows how bilingual children can benefit academically from opportunities to develop their biliterate skills. With case studies and examples of children's work, it shows how children's bilinguality provides opportunities for the development of literacy throughout the curriculum.

Garcia, O. (2009) *Bilingual education in the 21st century: a global perspective*. Wiley-Blackwell. This inspiring book provides an overview of bilingual education theories and practices throughout the world. It questions assumptions regarding bilingual education, and proposes a new theoretical framework for teaching and assessment of bilingual learners. It explains why bilingual education is good for all children throughout the world, and gives examples of successful bilingual programmes.

Gonzalez, N., Moll, L. and Amanti, C. (eds) (2005) *Funds of knowledge: theorizing practices in households, communities and classrooms*. New York: Routledge.
The concept of 'funds of knowledge' is based on the premise that people have valuable knowledge formed from their life experiences. This book gives readers the basic methodology of funds of knowledge research and explores its applications to classroom practice. It argues that instruction must be linked to students' lives, and that effective pedagogy should be linked to local histories and community contexts.

Gregory, E. (2008) *Learning to read in a new language: making sense of words and worlds*. London: Sage.
This book introduces an 'Inside-Out' (starting from experience) and 'Outside-In' (starting from literature) approach to teaching children to read. It draws on examples of children from a variety of different countries engaged in learning to read nursery rhymes and songs, storybooks, letters, the Bible, and the Qur'an, in languages they do not speak fluently. It argues that there is no universal method to teach children to read, but rather a shared aim which they all aspire to: making sense of a new world through new words.

Nieto, S. (1999) *The light in their eyes: creating multicultural learning communities*. New York: Teachers College Press.
Another inspiring book, which focuses on the significant role of teachers in transforming students' lives. It considers recent theories, policies, and practices about the variability in student learning and culturally responsive pedagogy and examines the importance of student and teacher voice in research and practice.

Wells, G. and Chang-Wells, G.L. (1992) *Constructing knowledge together: classrooms as centers of inquiry and literacy*. Portsmouth, NH: Heinemann.
The book focuses on literacy, providing case studies together with discussions of literary and sociocultural theories of learning and teaching. The examples of theory integrated with practice offer a framework for teachers to develop their own approaches to promoting literacy for their pupils.

Appendix 1: Model answers to the self-assessment questions

The learning review questions at the end of each chapter are, on the whole, very open, and there are no fixed answers for many of them. They are intended to help you reflect on the issues raised in the chapters, and develop your own professional understanding of them. The points given below help you to do this by suggesting possible factors you might consider.

Chapter 1: Introducing bilingual and EAL learners

1. This question is designed to get you to think about your own identity, and what matters to you as an individual, as this can sometimes become problematic when you are working with children from different language and cultural backgrounds. Traditionally, identity has been defined by broad, general factors such as gender, social background or ethnic group. But it may also be about features that are more personal to you, such as where you come from, your religion, your family circumstances, the music you like, the football team you support and so on. Think about times when you might have felt annoyed, upset or threatened because of something that was important personally to you.

2. This question is designed to get you to think about specific out-of-school factors that may impinge on children's learning. These may relate to issues connected with the family's home circumstances, or there could be things which, if you knew about them, were important in helping to promote their learning and academic success, e.g. literacy skills in another language.

3. This question is designed to get you to reflect on the choices teachers can make in dealing with individual children. There are no fixed answers, and in many circumstances no 'right' ways to behave as a teacher. But what you have read in this book may have helped you to consider some principled ways of understanding children's progress more widely than simply through what is happening in the classroom. For example, Umaru's teacher(s) might have tried to find out more about Sierra Leone than the fact that there was a war and some awful things happened.

4. Again, no fixed answers here, but try writing your vignette based on the models given in the chapter. When you have done so, you could share it with colleagues or classmates to widen your awareness of bilingual and EAL learners.

Chapter 2: All about language

1. The main implications of sociocultural theories and the ZPD are about the kinds of activities that will offer the greatest opportunities for learning. These clearly need to focus on speaking and listening, and involve children in using talk in a wide range of ways, with plenty of time devoted to small-group discussion-type activities. The progression in cognitive demand also needs to be considered, so medium-term planning is important in order to ensure that the learning objectives become increasingly demanding. At the same time, contextual support needs to be maintained. Look back at the examples of planning given on pages 57–61.

2. The main differences are to do with what the grammars encompass and what their purposes are. Most conventional grammars consider words and perhaps sentences. They deal with semantics (meanings), morphology (grammar within words – the morphemes with which words are made up) and syntax (the order of words in sentences). Functional grammars, on the other hand, consider whole texts and the ways that words and sentences are used in their construction, according to the purposes and audiences of the text and the content it is intended to communicate. Functional grammars are more about understanding languages as part of culture and society and conventional grammars are more about describing languages as systems without reference to their social and cultural contexts.

3. Sociocultural theories argue that interaction, through talk as well as other means, is at the centre of the learning process. They emphasise the importance of making oral language a central aspect of all the learning that children are expected to do in primary schools, no matter what the subject or conceptual learning involved.

4. For the reasons given above, i.e. that it is through engaging in activities that focus on oral language that children will learn most effectively. This is a key conclusion of the *National Curriculum Review* (2011), which contains many useful references to support the development of your understanding in this area.

Chapter 3: What does it mean to be bilingual?

1. This question obviously needs to be answered through reflecting on your own views and opinions. It would be useful, perhaps, if you reflected on what you thought about bilingualism before reading the chapter and what you thought about it after. The conventional view is that bilingualism is about having full competence in two or more languages, whereas the ideas expressed in the chapter are intended to help you to see it as a much more fluid, diffuse concept, including social and cultural aspects as well as language.

2. Again, the answer to this question depends very much on your own personal and educational experiences. Perhaps you could also make it the topic of a group discussion as part of developing your professional understanding about the role of language diversity and bilingualism in children's learning.

3. The answer to this question would include ideas such as using a wider range of ways of assessing learning than the usual writing-focused tasks, possibly using practical activities and perhaps visual means. There is also the possibility of assessing children's conceptual understanding of the particular subject content in their home languages.

Chapter 4: Planning across the curriculum for bilingual and EAL learners

As a means of reviewing the learning outcomes of this chapter, there is a planning checklist (page 67) which you could use to evaluate your planning for teaching and subject across the curriculum on your next placement.

Chapter 5: Strategies and resources for promoting learning across the curriculum

1. Another fairly open question, but the kinds of 'funds of knowledge' you might think about could relate to knowledge children might gain through taking part in family activities such as cooking, sewing, planning journeys, keeping in touch with relatives in other countries, etc.

2. Issues to consider here could be about the working relationships you need to develop in order to value the expertise your colleague has, recognising the extra time they may be putting in (e.g. if they are a TA, they may be working on part-time terms) and that they may not have had professional training.

3. Issues to consider here would be similar to those in question 2 in some ways, and in addition, you may come across some colleagues who do not recognise the need for working bilingually to enhance children's learning. But, with positive professional relationships, you can do a great deal through team teaching, joint planning and supporting each other in your work to play to each other's strengths.

Chapter 6: Assessing bilingual and EAL learners across the curriculum

1. The purpose of assessment *for* learning, sometimes known as formative or diagnostic assessment, is to find out what your learners can do and what they find difficult, in order to plan how to help them make further progress. Assessment *of* learning is the same as summative assessment, and its main purpose is to identify what point children have reached on an externally decided, standardised scale of attainment in order to assign levels or other external criteria. In assessing the achievements and attainment of EAL and bilingual learners,

the distinctive nature of their language development and learning always has to be borne in mind.

2. The main reason is that if we do confuse *learning needs* and *language needs* for bilingual and EAL learners, we will not be able to make the appropriate provision to help them make progress and succeed.

3. AfL processes are very valuable for bilingual and EAL learners as they offer a range of ways to find out about their learning more holistically. Using the NALDIC EAL descriptors (see page 99) will enable you to reach a deep understanding of a child's strengths and needs, and what to do to help them make progress. The issues faced in sampling the work of a child who is relatively new to English are, of course, to do with communication. The child may not understand what is expected of her or him; there may be cultural issues in the task that you are not aware of and finally the child may understand the concept under consideration, but not have enough English to express or explain it in a way that is comprehensible to you

4. The main point here is to recognise that parents from different cultural backgrounds may express their concerns and interest in their children's progress in different ways. Sometimes, Asian-heritage parents can appear passive as they do not question their child's teacher or engage in discussion. This may be because they see the teacher as the authority figure, and their role as to support what the teacher says, rather than agree or disagree with it.

Appendix 2: Glossary

Academic language Academic language is the kind of language that learners need to understand and use in order to carry out cognitively complex activities and to achieve success academically. It is used in textbooks, in tests and in formal classroom discourse.

Accent Accent refers to the ways people pronounce the languages they speak. Accents can be specific to a country, a region, a town or city, a social group or an individual. Speakers of English have many different accents according to where they come from and their social and cultural backgrounds.

Achievement An assessment of achievement reveals the knowledge, skills, understandings and capabilities of a learner, as well as the progress they are making compared with learners of similar capability.

Additive bilingualism Additive bilingualism is where the acquisition of a new language does not replace the first language; instead the first language is promoted and developed. It is linked to high self-esteem, and improved cognitive flexibility.

Attainment Attainment is a measure of how well a learner is performing in a particular subject, linked to an external set of criteria, such as the National Curriculum Attainment Targets.

Authentic language Contrasted with the language used in many school textbooks, curriculum programmes and teaching resources, authentic language is the kind of language that people use in their everyday lives to do the things they want to do.

BICS (basic interpersonal communication skills) Cummins made a distinction between two kinds of language knowledge and proficiency (see CALP below). BICS refers to the conversational fluency that most learners of a new language can develop relatively quickly in everyday social interactions.

Bilingual A word with many definitions; in this book, it refers to anyone who has access to and uses more than one language in their everyday life.

Codeswitching Codeswitching refers to a speaker's use of more than one language in one utterance or conversation. It is a natural and normal aspect of the speech of many bilingual people.

CALP (cognitive academic language proficiency) CALP is the second type of language understanding knowledge and skill that Cummins identified in his research (see BICS above). CALP is associated with academic learning and is the language of cognitive processes such as analysing, synthesising, arguing and persuading.

Cognitive language Cognitive language is the kind of language required to engage in cognitively challenging activities, e.g. Latinate words, complex grammatical structures and long, tightly-structured texts.

Context of use Part of the functional grammar approach, the context of use of a text is the set of social and cultural factors which surround it and contribute to its construction, i.e. why, when, how and where it was produced (the purposes), who it was produced for (the audience) and what it is about (the content).

CUP (common underlying proficiency) CUP relates to Cummins' theories of bilingualism and is a term to describe the ways in which our processing of language is supported by all the languages we know. Rather than possibly 'interfering' with each other, knowledge of different languages feeds into a common 'reservoir' of knowledge, understanding and capacity to express meaning.

DARTS (directed activities related to texts) DARTs are activities that encourage the learner to analyse how a text is constructed and how its meanings are expressed at word, sentence and text level. There are two types: 'disruption' activities where the learner is expected to alter the text in some way, e.g. changing the tenses, and 're-construction' activities, such as a cloze activity.

Dialect Dialects are the varieties of a language in terms of grammar and vocabulary. English has many different dialects, both regional within Britain and international across the globe.

EAL (English as an additional language) EAL is a term used to refer to those children in the education system who speak, and possibly read and write, other languages besides English. The term EAL is now increasingly used to identify a distinctive 'field' of language teaching and learning.

EFL (English as a foreign language) EFL refers to the branch of English language teaching and learning concerned with teaching people from other countries who plan to live, work or travel in England (see TEFL below).

ELT (English language teaching) A broad term used to cover the range of fields of English language teaching and learning.

Functional approach (to grammar) The functional approach to grammar is one which considers whole texts (either spoken or written) in their contexts of use (see above) and the choices the speaker or writer has made in constructing them.

Funds of knowledge 'Funds of knowledge' refers to the learning, often social and cultural and sometimes academic, which a child engages in within their home and community contexts, and which they bring to school.

Genre Genres are different text types, defined by the purposes and audiences for which they are intended and the kinds of language and structural elements with which they have been constructed.

Grammar Grammars are systematic ways of describing languages. There are many different kinds of grammars, which each pay attention to different aspects and elements of language.

Halal Anything which is halal is acceptable within Islamic rules and standards. Something which does not meet these standards is defined as *haram*.

Heritage languages In England, the term 'heritage languages' normally refers to the languages of the country of origin, spoken by people who have migrated to England, or whose ancestors did so.

Hot seating Hot seating is a technique used in drama and role play where a participant is asked to sit on a chair in the role of a character, e.g. from a story or from a historical period, and answer questions put to them by the audience in that role. It is a valuable teaching strategy in different subjects across the curriculum.

Identity The word 'identity' is used in many different ways to describe an individual's sense of who they are, where they belong and how they would define themselves.

Jigsawing Jigsawing is a technique used in discussion-based activities where participants each have partial information about the topic under consideration and they have to collaborate in different ways in order to disclose the full information.

KWL (know, want to find out, learn) grid A KWL grid can be used in various ways, to help in planning a project or introducing a new topic in teaching.

KWHL (know, want to find out, how to find out, learn) grid An extension of KWL, and a useful device in lesson or activity planning.

Linguistic interdependence Another of Cummins' theories, linguistic independence refers to the idea that knowledge and understanding of one language links to and supports the development of knowledge and understanding in another.

Metalinguistic awareness Metalinguistic awareness is the deeper understanding of how languages work as systems and the capacity to explain them, gained from studying and analysing languages, and comparing different languages.

Monolingualising Monolingualising is a term introduced by some researchers to describe the way that the curriculum can impose a message that English is the only language that matters, and that other languages are much less important.

Multi-modal Texts which are multi-modal are constructed with a mix of forms, usually including aural and visual elements, and also conventional text forms.

Multiliterate The capacity to read and/or write more than one language, at any level.

National Association for Language Development in the Curriculum (NALDIC) NALDIC is the national subject association for English as an additional language (EAL). It was founded in 1992 and is recognised today as the foremost organisation promoting effective teaching and learning for bilingual and EAL children in schools in the UK.

Received pronunciation (RP) RP is the prestigious form of pronunciation of English that is associated with high status and educational success. Traditionally, it is the way of speaking that had to be adopted by members of society who wished to be received in court.

Repertoire Repertoire refers to the whole range of knowledge about languages an individual possesses, in terms of listening, speaking, reading and writing. It can change many times over an individual's life course, according to a wide range of social, cultural, academic and personal factors.

SATs (standardised assessment tasks) SATs are the tasks in English and maths, commissioned by the government, to identify and record the attainment of children at the age of 7 (KS1) and 11 (KS2).

Scaffolding Scaffolding is an idea (sometimes called a 'theory of instruction') that goes along with the notion of the ZPD (see below). It refers to an approach to planning activities in order to offer learners opportunities to acquire new knowledge securely while at the same time developing as independent learners.

SLA (second language acquisition) SLA is the process of developing the skills and knowledge to communicate in an additional language, as distinct from the knowledge that might be learnt through direct teaching.

Semantics Semantics is the part of language knowledge and study to do with meaning in words, sentences and whole texts.

Standard English Standard English is the high-status form of English grammar and vocabulary associated with educational and economic success, spoken by people in England. For many people, it is one of several kinds of English they have in their repertoires. People speak standard English with a wide range of regional and social accents.

Superdiverse Superdiverse is a term from sociology to describe contemporary societies where migration over many years has led to complex communities whose members possess an increasingly wide range of language, cultural, social and economic backgrounds.

TEFL (teaching English as a foreign language) TEFL is a pedagogy for teaching English to people who wish to live in, work in or visit Britain and other English-speaking countries. It is often carried out before the learners travel, and can also take place in short courses in the English-speaking host country.

Texts Texts can be either spoken or written. They are complete, communicative events transacted through language that has been selected to take account of the speaker(s)' or writer(s)' purposes, meanings and audiences.

Transitional bilingualism Transitional bilingualism is a contrasting term to additive bilingualism (see above). It describes the situation where an individual, in acquiring a new language, loses their capacity to use existing languages in their repertoires. It is associated with low levels of academic attainment and success.

Translanguaging Translanguaging is a recently developed term used to describe the ways that multilinguals make choices from their language repertoires to express their meanings and perform their identities in the ways most appropriate to them. Unlike the term 'codeswitching' (see above), it helps us to consider languages as fluid and seamless, rather than as separate and isolated systems.

ZPD (zone of proximal development) The idea of the ZPD comes from Vygotsky's theories about learning as a sociocultural process, in which the interactions between learners and their teachers are an important element. The ZPD is Vygotsky's term to describe the 'gap' between what the learner knows and what they do not yet know, which can be bridged with the support of a more knowledgeable other.

Appendix 3: Principles for planning for bilingual learners

These six key principles for planning lessons and activities for bilingual learners have been developed from the ideas discussed in Chapters 1 to 3. In Chapters 4 to 6, I use these principles to present practical examples of activities and strategies to promote bilingual children's learning in speaking and listening, reading and writing across the curriculum.

1. Developing a positive ethos that reflects language and cultural diversity at whole-school level supports home-school links, and encourages families and schools to work in partnership.

2. In the classroom, providing opportunities for bilingual pupils to use their first languages in everyday activities opens out potential for learning and affirms their identities.

3. Pupils need every possible opportunity to explore ideas and concepts orally in all subjects across the curriculum.

4. Before beginning extended writing activities, pupils need plenty of chances for collaborative discussion and practical experience.

5. Promoting awareness of language systems and structures by allowing bilingual pupils to analyse and compare the different ways of saying things in the languages they know helps develop their CALP and also promotes language awareness among their monolingual classmates.

6. Providing extensive opportunities for hands-on experience enhances language learning and learning more generally.

Index

Added to a page number 'f' denotes a figure and 'g' denotes glossary.